My FUJIFILM INSTAX MINI 8 INSTANT CAMERA FUN GUIDE!

101 Ideas, Games, Tips and Tricks For Weddings, Parties, Travel, Fun and Adventure!

By

Leslie Cameron

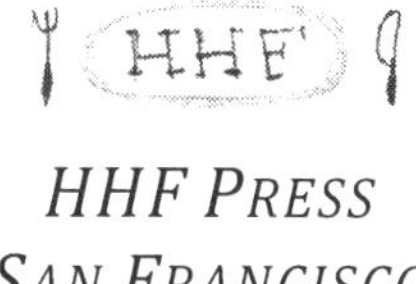

HHF Press
San Francisco

Legal Notice

The information contained in this book is for entertainment purposes only. The content represents the opinion of the author and is based on the author's personal experience and observations. The author does not assume any liability whatsoever for the use of or inability to use any or all information contained in this book, and accepts no responsibility for any loss or damages of any kind that may be incurred by the reader as a result of actions arising from the use of information in this book. Use this information at your own risk.

The author reserves the right to make any changes he or she deems necessary to future versions of the publication to ensure its accuracy.

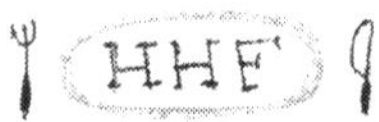

DO YOU LIKE FREE BOOKS?

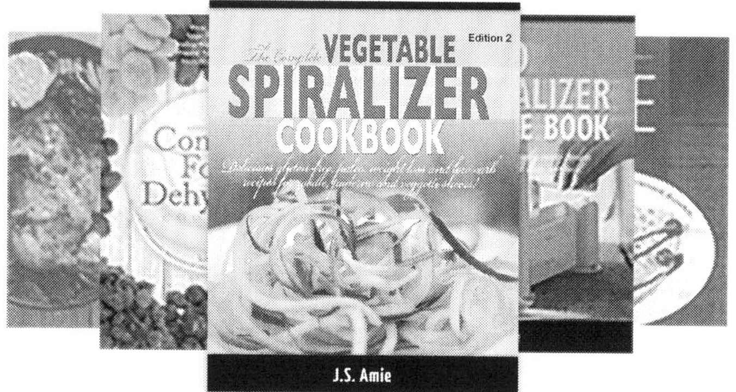

Every month we release a new book, and we offer it to our current readers first…absolutely free! This helps us get early feedback before launching a book, and lets you stock your shelf full of interesting and valuable books for free!

Some recent titles include:

- The Complete Vegetable Spiralizer Cookbook
- My Lodge Cast Iron Skillet Cookbook
- 101 The New Crepes Cookbook

To receive this month's free book, just go to

http://www.healthyhappyfoodie.org/v1-freebooks

Table Of Contents

1

Why You Need This Book

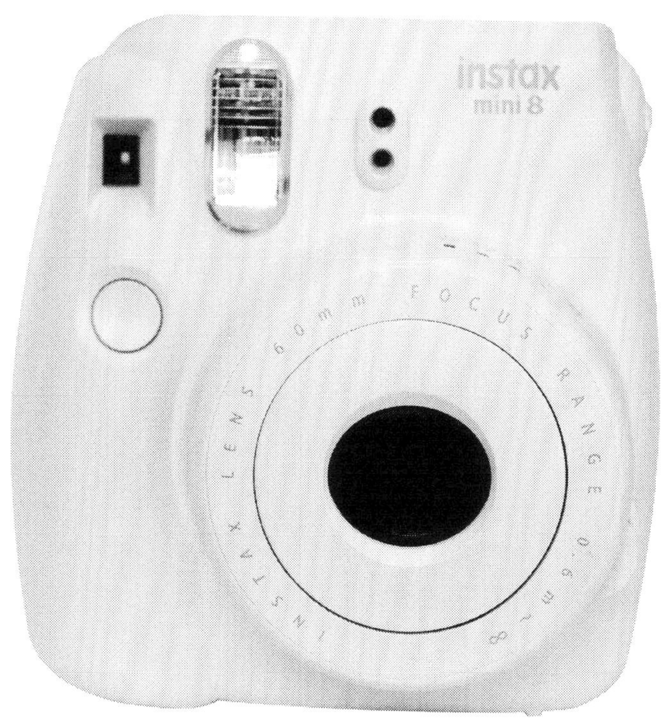

It's The ONLY Book Written Specifically for The Instax Mini 8

The Instax Mini 8 is a great way to take pictures on the go and develop them in seconds. With seemingly limitless uses, the Mini 8 is perfect for parties, travel, and art projects, and this book will teach you everything you need in order to maximize your Instax Mini 8's full potential. We will cover how to properly use the camera, including the best methods for loading and developing the film, to helpful tips about how to frame photographs, and use the different lighting settings to get perfect pictures every time.

This book will turn you into an expert in no time so that you can get to work taking fun and artistic pictures wherever you go. Along the way, we'll discuss the history of instant cameras and why they have remained so popular over the years. We'll also go into why the Instax camera is the best option for photographers looking to make instant prints that are crystal clear and full of vibrant colors.

Unlock Your Instax's Potential to Take Great Pictures

Many cameras are capable of taking great pictures, but knowing how to properly use the equipment can be the difference between an ok picture and a great one. We will discuss the techniques you will need to learn in order to take the best possible pictures every time.

The Instax Mini 8 is designed to be easy to use, extremely durable, and most of all, fun. But knowing how to properly use the lens settings can make all the difference. Luckily, your Instax Mini 8 has a built in sensor to take some of the guess work out of this. Much like professional SLR type cameras, the Instax Mini 8 features a lens that has a variable aperture.

This means that you can adjust the amount of light that enters the camera based on the conditions you're in. By adjusting the lens dial to suit the amount of light in your environment, you can control how much light enters the camera. This feature allows you to ensure that your photos will never be too bright or too dark.

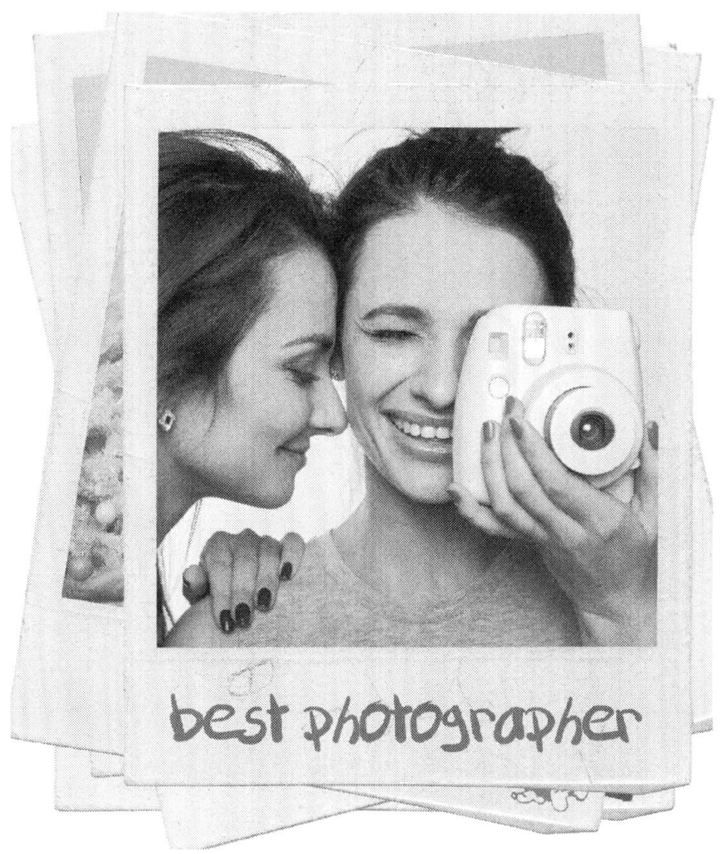

Amazing Pro Tips for Taking the Best Possible Pictures

In this section, we will cover how to use different techniques to make the experience of using the Instax Mini 8 even more successful. From tips about manually controlling the flash to advice about framing your photos, we will cover everything you need to make your Instax photos even better. We will even go into tips on how to choose the perfect shooting distance to get the sharpest photos in perfect focus. And once you've taken and developed your pictures, we will give you some great ideas about how to use and display them in fun and different ways.

Over 100 Ideas for Fun Ways to Use the Instax Mini 8

These days we all take lots of pictures and the Instax Mini 8 is a fun and reliable way to take great vintage looking photos that develop in seconds. In this section, we will show you dozens of ideas for fun ways to use the Mini 8. From weddings to camping trips, and family vacations, the Mini 8 has so many potential uses that you will never run out of projects. In addition, showing you the many ways the Instax can be used to create great photos, we will also show you many fun ways to use the photos you've made. The Instax is perfect for collages and scrapbooks as well as holiday decorations and even jewelry.

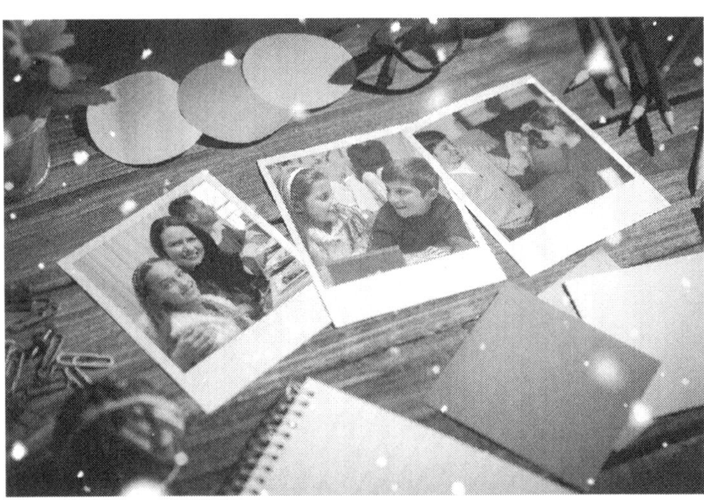

It's The Only Book About the Instax You Will Ever Need

Because this book covers every possible topic related to the Instax Mini 8, you can be assured that this guide will be the only book you will ever need in order to truly get the most out of your new camera. From our in depth, step-by-step guide to properly using the camera, to the best way to store the camera, we will cover everything you need to know in order to become an expert Instax photographer in no time.

2

Why Choose Instax

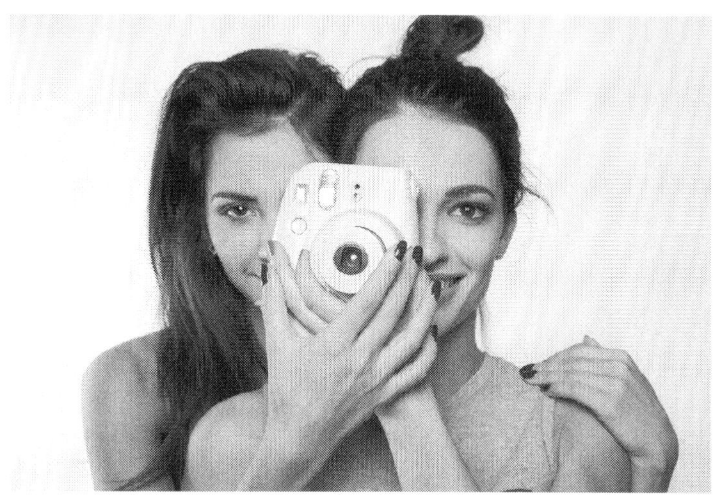

It's The Best Instant Camera on The Market

Instant cameras have existed for over fifty years, but many of them suffer from some serious disadvantages. Many of the cameras were fragile and not capable of producing high quality photos. The Instax is revolutionary because it is easy to use, versatile, durable, and best of all, takes great pictures. Perfect for adults and children, it is easy to learn to use the Instax and durable and small enough to travel with you anywhere. The Instax also uses features found on more expensive professional cameras to be the most versatile instant camera on the market. With its ability to shoot photos in high and low light, the Instax allows you to take pictures any time in any location. And since the Instax has become so popular with photography enthusiasts, the film is very easy to find.

Learn Techniques for Creating the Best Photos On the Go

Most of photography is learning techniques to control light and focus. The Instax is superior to other instant cameras because it gives you more control over these conditions. Many instant cameras have a fixed aperture that you cannot adjust depending on how bright it is. The problem with this is that too much light will result in over exposed, washed out photos, while too little light will produce dark photos. The key to controlling the light that enters the camera is the aperture control. In brighter conditions, the camera will sense the amount of light and automatically adjust the lens to let in less light and in darker conditions it will adjust to let in more light. This can also be controlled manually by adjusting the lens dial. We will learn more about how to use this feature later in the book.

It's The Fastest Way to Make Instant Prints

Part of the fun of instant cameras is being able to see the photos you've taken as soon as you take them. In the past, instant photos took a long time to properly develop and there was a lot of waiting time between taking a photo and seeing it. The Instax, on the other hand, uses film that develops far faster than other instant film so you can see the results almost instantly. Since the Instax is a great camera for kids, they won't need to wait for their photos to appear. Simply snap a picture and it will be visible in less than a minute.

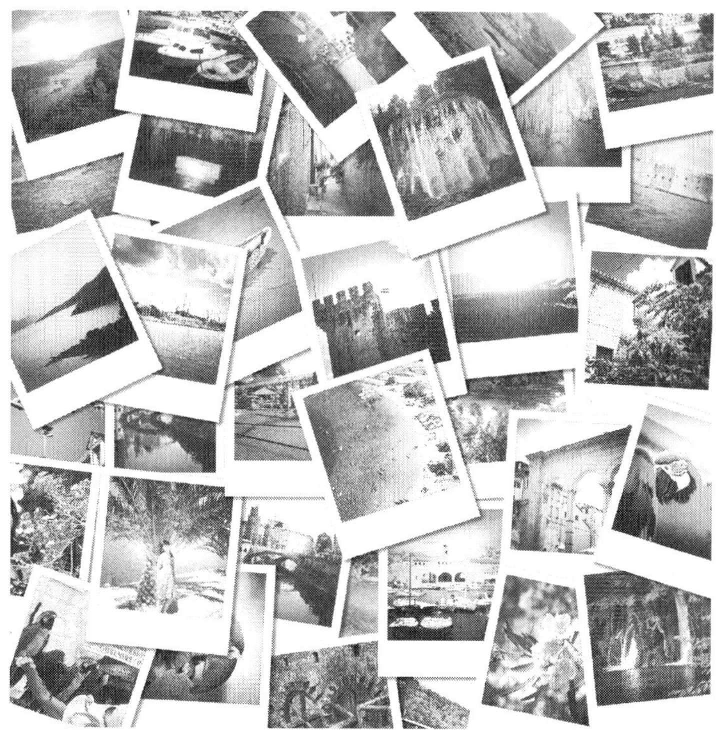

It's The Most Durable Instant Camera On the Market

Durability has always been an issue with instant cameras, but thanks to the Instax's modern you never have to worry that your camera will be too fragile to take anywhere. The camera is constructed from high quality plastic that will easily resist falls and the lens is positioned so that it is protected if the camera should fall. The Instax Mini 8 is designed so that it can be enjoyed by photographers of all ages. It is perfect for kids' parties and weddings, and because it is so sturdy, you never have to worry about accidentally dropping it.

It Comes in Seven Fun Colors

Everyone has their own style and the Instax is designed for every taste in seven different colors. Choose the color that suits your style and start taking great vintage pictures right away. Right now, the Instax Mini 8 comes in: white, yellow, pink, red, purple, blue and black. With so many choices every member of the family is sure to have a color that suits their unique style.

3

A Brief History of Instant Cameras

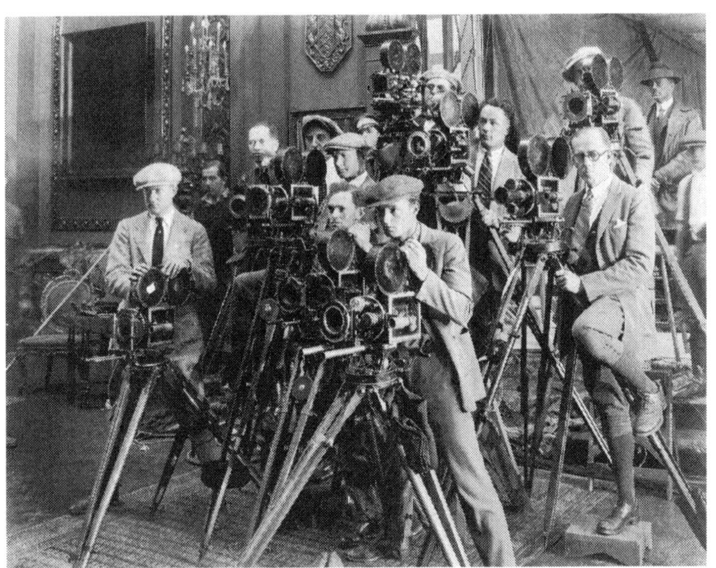

From The Polaroid to The Instax: A History of Instant Cameras

Instant cameras have existed since the late 1940's and have been rapidly changing ever since. The first instant cameras operated with a film roll system and were often very unreliable and difficult to use. However, once the Polaroid camera came onto the scene in the mid 1960's everything changed. The original cameras were often large, bulky, and not meant to be moved around. They were mostly used for things like passport photos and for police purposes, but when Polaroid developed a small, compact camera along with a film cartridge system that was more stable, the instant photo industry really took off. Since the advent of digital cameras and smart phones, the use of instant cameras began to decline, but much like the resurgence of vinyl records, there is now a thriving demand for vintage style photography, specifically instant photos. The difference between Instax and its predecessors is that Instax has taken some of the features of more advanced cameras in order to make more reliable prints in all lighting conditions.

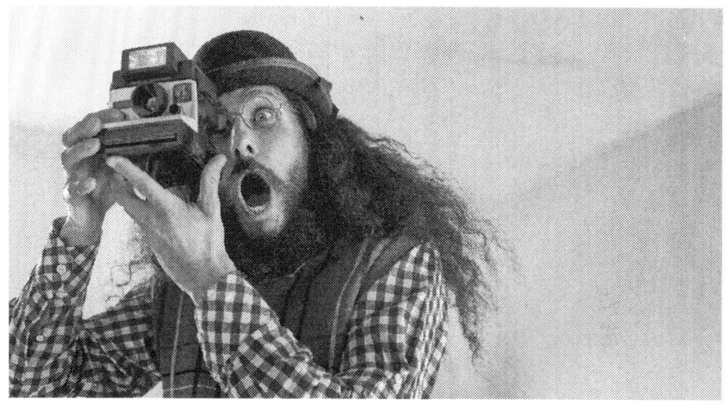

The Technology Behind Instax Film

So what makes Instax film different from other instant film? The most obvious difference is that it comes in a wide variety of fun frames, but the biggest difference is the technology behind the film. By using direct positive sign crystal emulsion technology, Instax film has one significant advantage over other instant film: it performs at a higher speed than other instant film. This means that it will work better in lower light conditions and, in general, be more versatile than other films. The main challenge faced by instant film in the past was that it worked well for bright daylight shooting, but was not very good for use indoors or at night. The combination of this technology along with the Mini 8's ability to adjust to different lighting conditions means that you can reliably shoot great photos with the Instax anywhere, and any time of day. The makers of Instax film also developed new technology to increase the speed at which the photos develop. This means no more waiting for your photos to develop.

Do More with The Instax Mini 8 than Any Other Instant Camera

We've already discussed the technology and history behind the instant camera, and why the Instax Mini 8 is an exciting new choice, but what really matter is what this allows you to do with your camera. Apart from film choices that allow for different sizes and colors, the camera itself is amazingly versatile. Since most instant cameras use a fixed light setting, it can be difficult to get good pictures in any condition other than bright sunlight. The Mini 8, however, features a useful light sensor that adjusts depending on the amount of light. Because of this sensor, the camera is able to adjust the lens to let in more or less light. This is a feature that more advanced camera has been using for a very long time, and the Mini 8 has finally brought it to instant photography.

Get Superior-Quality Pictures with The Instax Mini 8

One of the main drawbacks of instant cameras has always been the inferior picture quality. Photos are often either washed out, too dark, or have inaccurate colors. Thanks to the newly developed technology of Instax film, these are no longer problems when using instant cameras. The construction of the Mini 8's lens means better adjustment for different lighting conditions, and the revolutionary new Instax film means that colors are represented more accurately than ever before, and with greater focus and detail. For this reason, you get all of the vintage charm of instant photos but without any of the drawbacks. Instax film is also designed to be more chemically stable so those photos should retain their colors longer than traditional instant film.

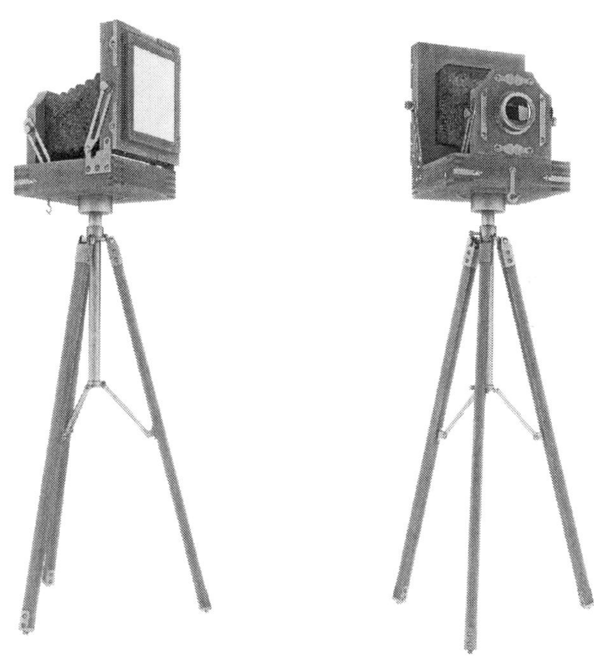

4

How to Use Your Instax Mini 8 Camera

Properly Setting Up Your Mini 8

As you'll see, setting up and using the Mini 8 really couldn't be easier. First, unpack all of the contents of the box. Two AA batteries are included, and the battery compartment is on the side of the camera. Once the batteries are in place, open the back of the camera. You will notice that there are yellow stickers on both the camera and the film. When inserting the film into the camera, make sure that the yellow stickers line up with each other. This means that the film is properly installed. Close the back of the camera and get ready to start taking pictures. First, turn on the camera by pressing the button located to the side of the lens. When the camera is on, a red light will become visible.

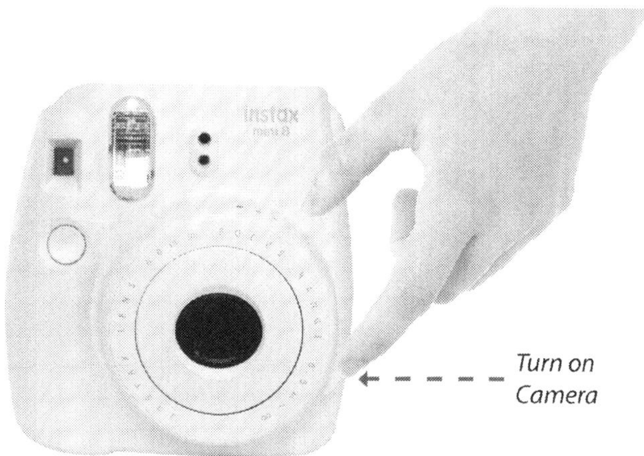

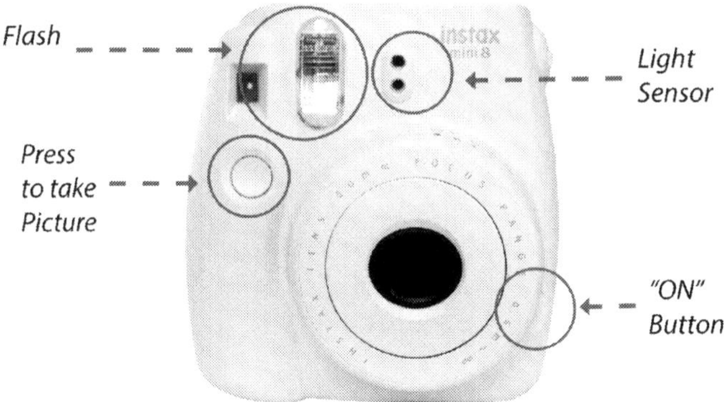

To take a picture, press the button on the top of the camera. It is important to note that the first time you press the button after loading a new cartridge of film a photo will not be produced. This is simply the cover that keeps the film protected from light. After that piece comes out you can begin taking pictures. You will notice two small holes at the top of the lens. These are the light sensors and will determine how much light is let into the camera. You can adjust the light setting to correspond with the light sensor simply by turning the lens to the correct setting. Take a picture and it will be ejected from the camera. The photo should develop in a very short time, but while it is developing, be careful not to shake the photo. Once you're finished taking pictures, push the lens back in to turn off the camera.

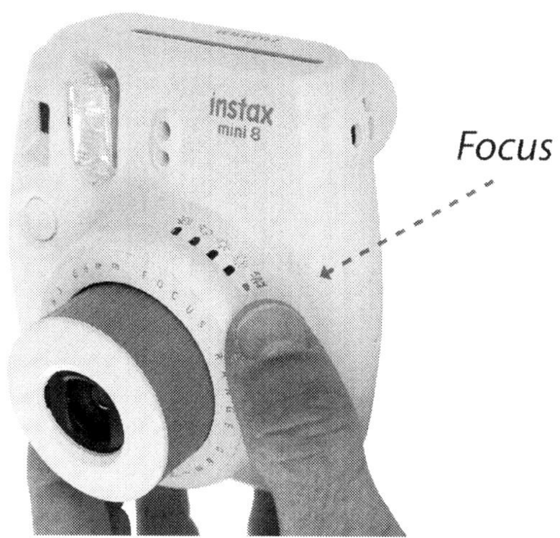

How to Use the Instax Film and Develop Pictures in No Time

The reason Instax film performs so much better than the competition is because it is easier to handle and more stable. The chemical technology behind Instax film means that it will stay fresh longer in order to produce higher quality photos. Installing the film is as easy as lining up the yellow tabs on the film with the yellow tabs on the camera. The Instax cartridge will only fit into the camera one way, so you never have to worry that you have loaded the film incorrectly. Instax film is also uniquely designed to develop faster than other instant film so you get to see your pictures almost immediately. And because of Instax's revolutionary technology, there is no need to shake pictures to get them to develop faster. In fact, for best results, don't shake the photos at all.

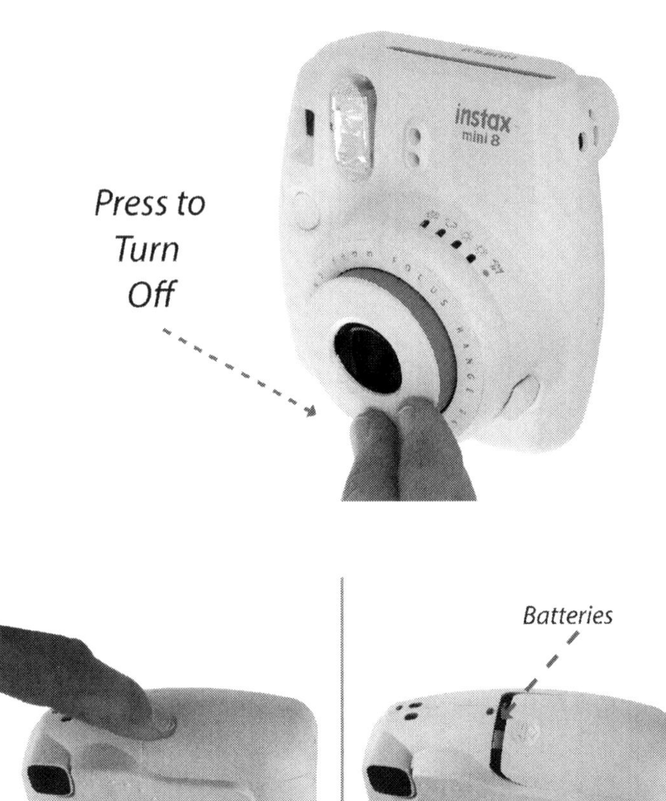

Press to
Turn
Off

Batteries

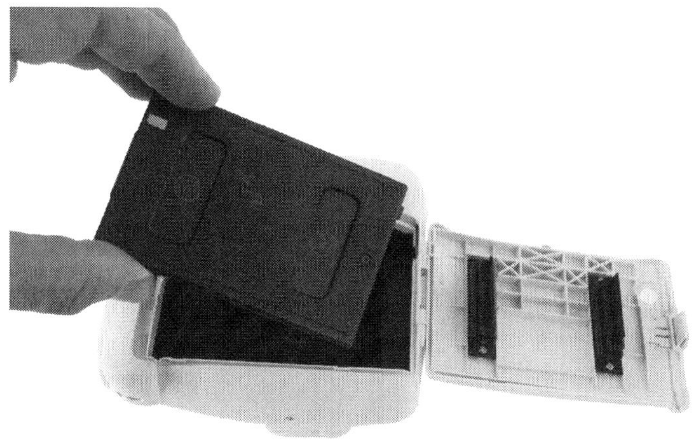

The Best Way to Use the Flash for Perfect Pictures

Since the Mini 8's flash is always activated, you never have to worry about whether or not you have remembered to turn it on. In lower light you can adjust the lens to allow more light to enter the camera, and this combined with the flash will guarantee that your photos never come out too dark. In daylight conditions, the flash may not be necessary, but it will not cause your photos to be over exposed because the lens will adjust to let less light in.

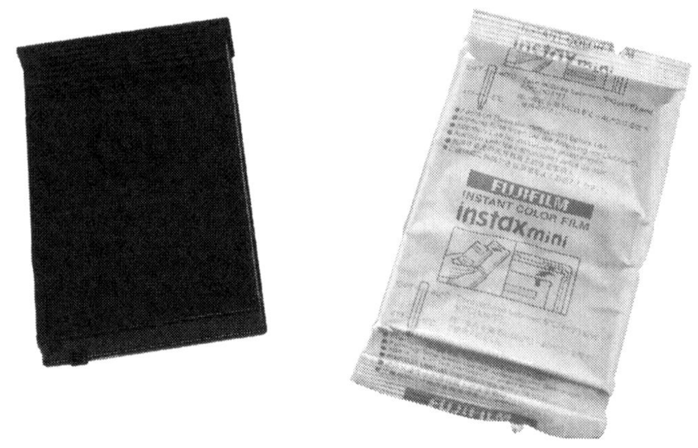

The Best Way to Store Your Instax Mini 8 for Travel

One of the best features of the Mini 8 is how durable it is. Because of this, traveling with the Mini 8 is easy and reliable. The camera is constructed from high quality plastic so it will be able to stand up to quite a bit of wear and tear. For best results while traveling with the camera, we recommend that the camera be stored without film as this can result in pictures being taken accidentally. Instax film is designed to withstand greater temperature changes than traditional instant film so there is no reason to worry about the film being ruined because of a large temperature change.

5

Pro Tips for Taking Perfect Pictures

Customize The Flash for Daylight Shooting

Since the flash on the Mini 8 is always on, you never need to worry if you have remembered to turn it on. However, there are times when you may not want a flash. In ordinary daylight conditions, the flash will most likely not affect the pictures, but if you do not want the flash we recommend using a small piece of electrical tape to cover the flash. Just make sure not to cover the light sensors next to the flash.

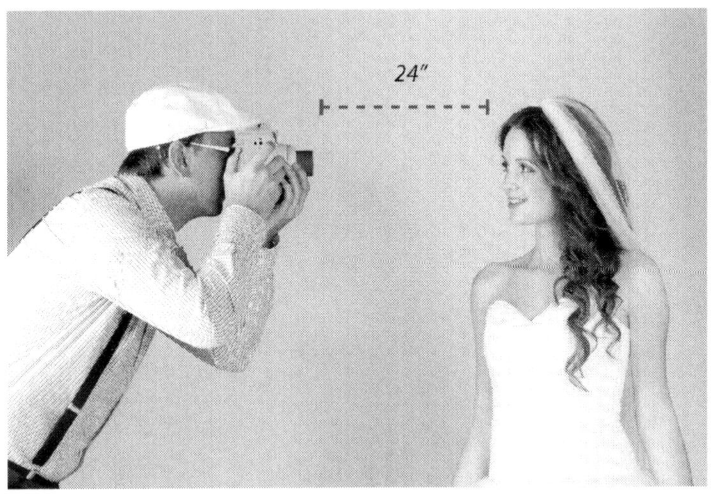

How to Shoot Pictures from The Optimal Distance

Like any camera, there are certain distances that the Mini 8 performs better at. While the Mini 8 is good for long distance shooting, shooting too close can result in a lack of focus. For best results, it is recommended that you leave a distance of about 24 inches between the camera's lens and whatever you want to take a picture of. Any closer and the subject may not be in perfect focus

How to Frame Your Photos Perfectly Every Time

Since the Mini 8 doesn't use a single lens reflex system, the viewfinder is not exactly the same image as what is captured by the lens. In order to accurately frame your photos, position the lens so that it is slightly up and to the right of what you see in the viewfinder. Keeping this simple tip in mind will allow you to center your images perfectly every time.

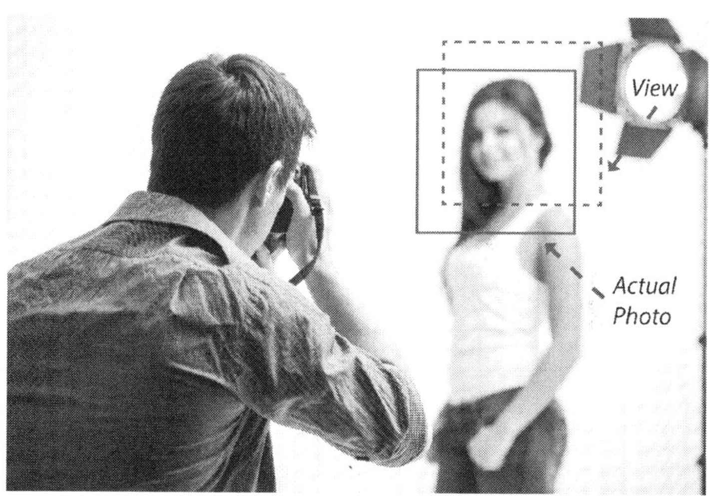

How to Get the Sharpest Photos from Your Instax

There are a couple of tips that can help you to avoid blurry pictures while using the Instax Mini 8. First, be sure to shoot your photos from an optimal distance. Too close and the camera will not be able to focus properly. Second, it is important to use film that has not expired. Expired film can lose definition as well as color quality. The third tip for getting clear pictures is to make sure your Mini 8 camera is kept clean inside and out. Dust and other debris can stick to the lens and create blurry photos. Likewise, dust can find its way inside the camera and stick to the film as you take pictures. This can result in pictures with spots or lack of focus.

Use your Photos in Lots of Fun Ways

Instax prints are about the size of a credit card so they are the perfect choice for scrapbooking or making collages. In addition to the white framed film, a wide varieties of fun colorful frame choices. Fuji Film is constantly introducing new frame options all the time. So in addition to putting you photos in the many different albums that are available for Instax photos, you can also experiment with ways of arranging the photos, or hanging them to create personalized decorations for any event. The Mini 8 is great for parties and is already a popular option for snapping wedding photos.

6

How to Keep Your Photos from Fading

The Best Ways to Store Your Photos to Avoid Fading

As with any type of photo, there are certain ways to ensure that your prints stay fresh and colorful for many years to come. The best way to keep Instax photos looking great it to make sure they are kept out of direct sunlight. There are lots of great ways to frame and display your photos, but be sure to keep them out of direct light. In addition to this, the other main factor in faded photos is heat. Rooms that get very hot for long periods of time are not the place to store photos as the chemicals in the prints will react with heat and result in changing, fading colors. For best results keep your Instax prints in albums. Speaking of which…

The Best Instax Photo Albums for Optimal Photo Storage

Instax prints can be stored in a wide variety of different albums, but there are albums that are made specifically for Instax prints. Since Instax prints are a different size than other instant photo, it is a great idea to purchase for albums that are sure to fit your prints. Albums are available in large traditional sized and since Instax photos are only about the size of a credit card, there are also an array of wallet sized albums made specifically for Instax mini prints, and are easy to take with you wherever you go. These albums will keep your prints safe and come in a wide variety of colors and styles.

Tips for Handling and Storing Instax Film for Best Results

Instax film isn't nearly as fragile as some other types of instant film, but there are still things that you can do to make sure that your prints come out perfectly every time. Keeping your camera clean is a great start, but you will also want to make sure that the film cartridges are free of dust or other debris so that it doesn't find it's way into the camera. This can lead to pictures with spots. If you plan to store your Instax film before using it, the best place to keep it is in the refrigerator. Since heat and temperature changes can cause film to have a shorter life span, keeping it in a cool place will keep the film fresh for longer and ensure that your photos will come out perfectly. If you are traveling with Instax film, it is a good idea to keep the film cartridges out of direct sunlight as this can make the chemicals within the film unstable, and result in poor quality pictures.

7

Wedding/Shower Ideas

Weddings and showers are once in a lifetime events that deserve to be captured in as many ways as possible. These are memories you will want to keep forever, and thanks to your Instax Mini 8, immortalizing these moments is something that the entire guest list can be a part of. In this section, we will give you some great ideas for how to get the most out of your Instax Mini 8 at weddings, and all types of showers. Of course, the Mini 8 can be used in so many ways that you will find yourself coming up with your own creative ideas in no time.

Instant Guest Book

Guest books have been a staple at weddings for as long as we can remember. Until recently, this meant that guests could sign their names upon arriving and offer some kind of message for the happy couple. But what if your guest book could be so much more than just a list of names and messages? What if those messages could be accompanied by the smiling faces of your guests?

What you will need:

Your Instax Mini 8 and enough film to capture all of your guests.

Tip: It's good to have a little extra film in case not every photo comes out just right.

A large ring binder

Heavy stock paper

Double sided tape

Some colorful magic markers

Instructions:

1. Load a cartridge of film into your Instax Mini 8. Make sure you have lots of extra cartridges around in case the guests show up quickly.

2. Put the paper into the ring binder and make the magic markers available.

3. Assign a good friend to stand with the guest book as your guest arrive.

4. As the guest arrive, have your friend snap a picture of each guest or couple.

5. Attach a piece of double sided tape to the back of the Instax picture and stick it to the guest book. Then give the guest a marker and let the write a personalized message next to their picture.

6. Now, whenever the newlyweds look at their wedding guest book they will see the smiling faces of all their guests as they read their well wishes.

Photo Booth

The photo booth is quickly becoming a staple of modern weddings, and while photography has played a large part in weddings ever since its invention, the focus has always been on the bride and groom and the rest of the wedding party. But the fact is, weddings aren't just about the couple who are getting married. They are also a way of bringing together family and friends to celebrate a special occasion. For this reason, having a way for your guests to commemorate the event is also very important. You can opt for an expensive photo booth, or you can use your Instax Mini 8 to make things much easier.

What you will need:

Your Instax Mini 8 and plenty of film

A table

Colorful magic markers

Instructions:

---

1. First, load your Instax Mini 8 with film and make sure to have plenty of extra cartridges on hand.

2. Choose a location that offers a fun background. Also, try to choose a location that has a decent amount of light.

3. Set your table up and if you would like, add a sign that lets your guests know that this is the photo booth.

4.   Guests can then take pictures of their friends and family throughout the event and use the markers to label each picture.

Candids for The Bride and Groom, Guests

Chances are, you will have a professional photographer at your wedding and they will, no doubt, take many beautiful pictures of the day. However, it can also be a great idea to let your friends and family join in on the photography. After all, these are the people who know you the best and they probably know how to find the perfect moments to capture your special day. The Instax Mini 8 makes this easy because it is so easy to use, and it reliably creates excellent quality pictures that can be enjoyed instantly.

What you will need:

Your Instax Mini 8 and lots of extra film
Your friends and family

Instructions:

---

1. Load your Instax Mini 8 with film and encourage your guests to pass the camera around. This can even work as a game.

2. Simply tell all of the guests that you want them to each take a photo of the wedding and write their names on the bottom of each picture so that the bride and groom will know who took it.

3. Since these are the people who know you the best, their pictures will be even more special.

Wedding/ Shower Scrapbook

Your Instax Mini 8 is a great way to capture a wedding or shower from every angle, but what do you do with the many pictures once the event is over? Since Instax prints are so easy to work with, creating a scrapbook from your wedding and shower is a great way to keep those pictures organized so that they can be enjoyed for years to come. This is a great way to commemorate weddings and showers, but it's also a great way to use your Instax pictures from any special event, from a Bar Mitzvah or graduation, to a senior prom or a special vacation.

What you will need:

Your Instax pictures

A colorful three ring binder with lots of pages

Double sided tape or a glue stick

Magic markers

Any other decorations that fit the theme of your scrapbook

Instructions:

1. First decide the order in which you would like to arrange your pictures. For wedding scrapbooks, it might make the most sense to start with pictures of the guests arriving and the wedding party getting ready. Then move along to the ceremony and festivities after the ceremony. Your scrapbook can tell the story of a special time in your life; a time that you will want to remember forever.

2.   Attach the pictures to the pages of the binder however you would like and use the markers to make notes about who is in the pictures and what they mean to you.

Welcome Sign

A great way to greet your guests and let them know they're in the right place is by having a festive welcome sign. Your Instax Mini 8 can help you create a personalized sign that will be the perfect introduction to your special event.

What your will need:

Your Instax Mini 8 and lots of film

A large piece of poster board

Double sided tape or a glue stick

Instructions:

1. First, gather all of the pictures that you have taken with your Instax Mini 8 that you would like to use to the sign.

2. If you've been using your Mini 8 to document your relationship, you can start the lettering with pictures from early on and tell the story of your relationship as you go.

3. You will need to have enough pictures to spell out whatever message you want. Then, use the pictures to spell out words such as: Welcome to Our Wedding!

4. Simply apply some glue or double sided tape to the backs of the pictures and arrange them into words.

Candids at Bachelor or Bachelorette Party!

The bachelor or bachelorette party has transformed in recent years from a single evening out on the town to often an entire weekend of fun. This means more things to document with your Instax Mini 8. If you are throwing a bachelor or bachelorette for a friend, Instax instant prints can be a great way to capture candid moments to compile into a special album.

What you will need:

Your Instax Mini 8 and plenty of film

A festive three ring binder or photo album

Double sided tape or a glue stick

Instructions:

---

1. Take plenty of photos at your bachelor/bachelorette party.

2. Choose the best photos that tell the story of the event and put them in order. Then place double sided tape or glue on the backs of the pictures and affix them to the pages of the album.

3. Since these parties usually take place well in advance of the wedding, the album can be a wonderful gift to be presented to the happy couple at the wedding.

Bachelorette Take Home: Photo Magnet of Guest and Bride to be

Your Instax Mini 8 is a great way of capturing moments, but it can also be a great way to make commemorative gifts for your guests. At many bachelorette parties it has become customary for the bride to give small gifts to the guests. One great simple gift is a magnet made from an Instax photo.

What you will need:

Your Instax Mini 8 and lots of film

Small round or square magnets

Strong holding glue

Magic markers

Instructions:

1. At the bachelorette party, take lots of photos, and be sure to get a photo of each guest with the bride.

2. Take all of the photos of a guest and the bride and, using some glue, affix the magnet to the back of the photo.

3. Allow the glue to dry and then use a marker to label each photo.

DIY Place Cards

If you're having a sit down dinner at your wedding, you have probably spent lots of time figuring out the seating chart. Once you've decided where everyone is going to sit, you will need place cards. One fun way of making your own do-it-yourself place cards is to use your Instax Mini 8. This way, when the guests make their way to the tables they will find a picture of themselves waiting on the table.

What you will need:

Your Instax Mini 8 and plenty of film

Blank A-frame place cards

Double sided take or a glue stick

A thick tipped pen or marker

Instructions:

---

1. In the months leading up to the wedding, try to get photos of all of your guests using your Instax Mini 8. Try to frame them horizontally in the landscape mode.

2. Once you have finalized your seating chart, use tape or glue to affix each picture to one of the A-frame place cards. You can print the guest's name above or below the picture.

3. At the wedding, place the cards on the tables and watch as your guests are surprised that the photo you took of them greets them to their table.

Customized Thank You Cards

After the festivities are finished and the gifts have been opened, it's time to tell your guests that you appreciate them coming to your big day. Instead of using standard thank you cards, make your own using your Instax Mini 8. Your Instax pictures will help you create a meaningful thank you card that will show your personal connection to all of your guests.

What you will need:

Your Instax Mini 8 and plenty of film

Blank greeting cards or simple thank you cards

A glue stick

A custom made rubber stamp with your wedding logo (optional)

Pens or markers

Instructions:

1. At your wedding, take a picture with each guest or couple, using your Instax Mini 8.

2. When it's time to send out the thank you cards, take each picture and using a glue stick, affix the picture to the front of a blank greeting card, or if you are using a simple thank you card, affix the picture to the inside of the card.

3. Write a personalized message to your guests.

Baby Shower Message Book

A baby shower is all about gathering your closest friends and family to celebrate a new life coming into the world. Since it is such a special event, it is important to commemorate it for the future. A message book allows every guest at your shower to send a personal message to the soon to be born baby, and will serve as a lasting memory as the child gets older. And it's a great way for your treasured guests to send a message of hope and love to a new member of the family.

What you will need:

Your Instax Mini 8 and plenty of film

A festive three ring binder or photo album

Heavy stock paper

A glue stick

Pens or fine tipped markers

Instructions:

---

1. At the shower make sure to take a picture of every guest.

2. Invite each guest to write a message to the unborn baby.

3. After the shower, use a glue stick to attach a photo of each guest to the book next to their message. This way, when the child grows older they will be able to read the messages and see a picture of the person who wrote it.

8

Travel Ideas

Traveling is a great way to learn about ourselves as well as other cultures, and as we experience new places there are always so many things that we want to remember and keep with us after we return home. Luckily, your Instax Mini 8 is the perfect traveling companion because it is easy to use, and more durable than most other cameras. This section will explore the many ways that you can use your Instax Mini 8 while exploring the world, and fun ideas to use your pictures once you're back at home.

Instant Vacation Album

With the rise of digital photography, we have become accustomed to snapping pictures and then not having a physical photograph. But sometimes, being able to flip through photos with friends or family is more fun that scrolling through pictures on your phone. Your Mini 8 will allow you to have physical copies of your photos instantly so you can review them even before you get home.

What you will need:

Your Instax Mini 8 and plenty of film

A three-ring binder or photo album

A glue stick or double sided tape

A pen or marker

Instructions:

1. As you travel, take pictures with your Mini 8.

2. At the end of each day, use tape or glue to affix your pictures into the album. This way you can keep track of your memories while you're still making them.

3. Instead of having a bunch of random photos at the end of your vacation, you can create a story as you travel the world. When you get home you can go back to your album and relive your adventure over and over.

Album of Landmarks

Depending one where you're traveling to, you may have decided on some specific landmarks that you want to visit. This project can work as a fun reminder of all the things you want to do on your vacation, or it can be a fun scavenger hunt with the goal being to find as many of the landmarks on your list as you can.

What you will need:

Your Instax Mini 8 and plenty of film

A three-ring binder or photo album

Double sided tape or a glue stick

Pens or markers

Instructions:

1. Before you leave, choose a list of landmarks that you would like to visit.

2. In the pages of your album, reserve a spot for each landmark with enough room for an Instax photo.

3. While on your trip, try to located landmarks and photograph as many landmarks as you can with your Mini 8.

4. Either when you return home, or at the end of each day of your trip, match the photos with the entry in your album and affix it with tape or glue.

Wine Tasting Journal

Wine tasting is certainly a fun way to spend an afternoon or a whole vacation. But after a few glasses at a few different vineyards it can be a bit... difficult to remember exactly what you've tasted.   In order to keep track of the different varietals and vintages why not use your Instax Mini 8 to keep track of what you're drinking and then compile a history of your vinous adventures.

What you will need:

Your Instax Mini 8 and plenty of film

Three ring-binder or other photo album

Double sided tape or glue stick

Pens or permanent magic markers

Instructions:

---

1. While wine tasting, use your Mini 8 to snap a picture of each bottle that you taste, making sure to get a close shot of the labels on the bottles.

2. After wine tasting, apply tape or glue to the back side of the photos and affix them to your album.

3. Beneath each photo write the name of the vineyard, variety of wine, vintage, and the date you tasted it. You can also add a rating to each type of wine so that you will know what you enjoyed for future purchases, and what you would rather not taste again.

Make Custom Luggage Tags

Traveling can be a wonderful experience, but there are certain aspects that can be stressful. In particular, dealing with a busy airport can be a challenge. Much of the stress of this situation is caused by having to keep track of our luggage. These days, many bags appear very similar and so it can be difficult to spot your bag at baggage claim. Even luggage tags can be deceiving. Thanks to the Mini 8 though, you can be sure you've picked up the right bag because it has a tag with your picture on it.

What you will need:

Your Instax Mini 8 and enough film to take pictures of your family.

A pen or magic marker

Clear, plastic luggage tag holders

Instructions:

1. Start by taking a picture of everyone who will be traveling.

2. Beneath the picture write the best contact number for this person in the event that the bag is lost.

3. Slide each picture into a luggage tag holder and attach to the corresponding bag.

Customized Wall Maps with Instax Travel Photos

One great part of traveling is keeping track of all of the places you've been. Whether you're a world traveler or just seeing as much of the USA as possible, it can be hard keeping track of everywhere you've been. Your Mini 8 can help because, in addition to being a great travel companion, you can snap easy pictures wherever you are and create a wall decoration that will show exactly where you've been.

What you will need:

Your Instax Mini 8 and plenty of film

A large wall hanging map

Thumb tacks or adhesive squares

Pens

Instructions:

1. First, you're going to need to do some traveling. If you've already traveled with you Mini 8 and have lots of pictures from different locals you have a head start.

2. Go through your photos and determine which photo was taken where. If you are planning to travel in the future, be sure to make a note of where your pictures are being taken as you go. The bottom space on Instax pictures is perfect for labeling.

3. Once you know where your pictures are from, locate the places on your map.

4. Using tacks or adhesive squares, attach the pictures to the map. Now you can see the extent of your travels, and the more you travel the more you can fill up you map with all of the places you've been.

Travel Memories Collage

If you've been using your Mini 8 to take pictures while traveling, you are probably looking for something to do with them once your trip is over. Creating a travel memories collage is a perfect way to commemorate a great trip.

What you will need:

Your Instax Mini 8 and plenty of film

A large poster board

Double sided tape

Other paper souvenirs from your trip

Instructions:

1. Organize all of your Instax photos from your trip and decide which ones you want to use.

2. Gather other paper souvenirs you kept from the trip. Things like interesting receipts or foreign money.

3. Use the double sided tape to attach your Instax photos and other souvenirs to the poster board.

Custom Post Cards

Post cards are a great way to show your loved ones that you've been thinking about them while you are traveling. With your Instax Mini 8 you can even make custom post cards that show your friends and family exactly what sights you've been seeing.

What you will need:

Your Instax Mini 8 and plenty of film

Index cards

Envelopes

Double sided tape

Pens

Instructions:

---

1. Choose some photos that you want to send to friends and family.

2. Using the double sided tape, attach pictures to the index cards. You should be able to fit about four photos to each card.

3. On the back of each card, write a message about your trip, and put the cards in envelopes. Address them and drop them off at the post office.

Food Journal

Let's face it, these days it seems like everyone is taking pictures of their food whenever they eat out. But if you're traveling in a new place, you are likely eating some new and interesting foods that you will want to remember later. Your Instax Mini 8 is great for taking quick snaps of your meals and you can use those pictures later to create a journal of all the interesting things you ate on your trip.

What you will need:

Your Instax Mini 8 and plenty of film

A photo album or three ring binder with heavy paper pages

Double sided tape

Pens

Instructions:

1. As you travel, make sure to take photos of the meals you eat in different locations.

2. On the blank space at the bottom of each photo, make a note about where you ate and what this particular dish is called.

3. When you've arrived home, attach the photos to your album or binder and write a brief note about your impressions of the meal. Now you can share your culinary experiences with friends and family and they will be able to see exactly what you ate.

Learn Foreign Words with Instax

If you're traveling in a foreign land where they speak another language, it can be helpful to learn some basic vocabulary to make getting around a little easier. In most countries the locals are pleased if tourists make the effort to learn a bit of their language. Your Instax Mini 8 can be very helpful by allowing you to make on the go language reminders that you can study back at the hotel.

What you will need:

Your Instax Mini 8 and plenty of film

A pen

Your smart phone

Instructions:

1. While you are traveling, take pictures of things you don't know how to say in the local language. These can be things like food items, store names, or simple things like public transportation and bathrooms.

2. Use your smart phone's translate function to find out how to say these things in the local language and write it in the blank space at the bottom on your photos.

3. You can study the photos to learn the words and phrases, or you can keep them with you while sightseeing so that you have an instant reference.

Contact Cards for New Friends

One of the best parts of traveling is meeting new people. Sometimes you will meet people that you want to stay in touch with later, and your Instax Mini 8 is perfect for making contact cards so you can share your information.

What you will need:

Your Instax Mini 8 and plenty of film

A pen

Instructions:

---

1. When you've made new friends while traveling, take a picture of them and have them write their email address on the blank space at the bottom of their photo.

2. Now you will have a photo of your new friend and a way to contact them. You can also have them take a photo of you, and write your own email address at the bottom so they can have your information.

9

Decoration Ideas

These days everyone wants their space to be unique and to reflect their own personality. From kids and teens all the way up to adults of all ages, we're not satisfied to have the same decorations as everyone else. Thanks to your Instax Mini 8 you can always stand out from the crowd with creative design projects that can reflect your current mood and tastes. This section will focus on creating unique items for around the house using your Instax pictures.

Themed Collages

Collage art is a great way to express you create voice and with your Instax Mini 8 camera you can create a multitude of themed collages using your Instax pictures. The themes are up to you, but some ideas include: Recent travel, this school year, concerts and other events, hobbies, friends, and many more.

What you will need:

Your Instax Mini 8 and plenty of film

Poster boards

Double sided tape or glue sticks

Colorful magic markers

Instructions:

---

1. Start by going out and taking lots of pictures of different topics.

2. Sort your photos into the categories you want to make collages from.

3. Arrange the pictures on the poster boards in whatever way you want.

4. Apply tape or glue to the backs of the pictures and firmly stick them in place.

5. Further decorate the empty spaces on the poster boards with descriptions of the pictures or memories from the events.

Vision Boards

A vision board is a great way to keep your goals in perspective. From moving up at a job, to getting the house of your dreams, it can be productive to have a visual representation of your goals to remind you to be striving for them every day. Of course, everyone has different goals so the first thing you will want to do is choose the things you want to achieve and then use your Instax Mini 8 to take pictures of them.

What you will need:

Your Instax Mini 8 and plenty of film

Poster board

Double sided tape or glue stick

Pens or magic marker

Instructions:

---

1. Use you Instax Mini 8 to take pictures that represent your goals. From a new house, to the family of your dreams and everything in between. There are no limits on your dreams

2. Arrange your photos into the basic order in which you would like to accomplish these things.

3. Apply tape or glue to the back of the photos and and affix them to the poster board in the order that you have chosen.

4. Write a brief description of your goals under the pictures.

Hanging Photos

Creating hanging photos is not just a great way to display your Instax photos, it's also a great way to make unique, eye catching art that is sure to start a conversation. There are a number of different ways to tackle this project, but we're going to start with a way to use an old picture frame for a new purpose.

What you will need:

Your Instax Mini 8 and plenty of film

A picture frame, preferably at least 18 inches on each side or larger.

Medium weight cotton string

Thumb tacks

Scissors

Mini clothes pins (available at most craft stores)

Instructions:

1. Either take some pictures using your Mini 8 or find pictures that you have already taken.

2. Place the picture frame face down and arrange the pictures in rows across the frame to determine how many pictures will fit into each row.

3. Once you know how many rows you're going to make, measure the string so that it goes across the frame with an extra inch on each side.

4. Cut the string and, using thumb tacks, attach the string to the frame.

5.   Stand the frame upright and lean it against something.

6.   Using the mini clothes pins, attach the pictures to the strings to form rows.

7.   Hang in a place where it is sure to get lots of attention!

Customized Calendar

There are several ways to have fun with calendars and your Instax Mini 8 pictures, but we're going to focus on a really fun and simply project to actually create a beautiful and personalized flip calendar that will reflect your unique personality.

What you will need:

---

12 Instax pictures that each reflect a certain month

A hole punch

3 brass hooks screws

2 pieces of balsa wood that are the same size

Hot glue gun with glue

Magic marker

14 blank cards that are about the same size as your Instax pictures

Instructions:

---

1. First, prepare your pictures by using a magic marker to write the name of each month at the bottom of the pictures.

2. Prepare the blank cards by numbering one stack 0-3 and the other stack 0-9.

3. Punch a single hole at the top of each picture and card.

4. Using the hot glue gun, attach one piece of balsa wood to the other so that one piece is standing vertically on the other one which is

horizontal. Wait for the glue to completely dry.

5. Screw the three hooks into the vertical piece of balsa wood so that they are at the top of the wood and evenly spaced across.

6. On the screw all the way to the left hang the stack of pictures with the names of the month.

7. Hand the cards that represent the days so that the cards marked 0-3 are on the middle hook and the cards marked 0-9 are on the right hook.

Have Fun with your Workspace

At home we all have plenty of control over what we want our personal space to look like, but sometimes the office needs a personal touch as well. Studies have shown that employees who are allowed or encouraged to personalize their work spaces tend to be happier and more productive at their jobs. While every workspace is different, this fun idea should work for most walls and cubicles.

What you will need:

Your Instax Mini 8 and plenty of film

Medium strength cotton string

Mini clothes pins

Thumb tacks

Instructions:

1. First, find all of the Instax pictures you would like to display in your office or workspace.

2. Cut three pieces of string that are each 18-24 inches long. All three pieces should be the same length. (if you want to hang more or fewer rows of pictures that's up to you.)

3. Use the mini thumb clothes pins to attach the photos to the strings.

4. Hang the strings of photos in your office or cubicle using the thumb tacks.

Instax Clock

This project is a perfect way to turn an old unused clock into a personalized piece of art using your Instax Mini 8 photos. Since this project can be accomplished in several different ways, we'll show you how you can use most hanging clocks to make a truly interesting conversation starter.

What you will need:

Your Instax Mini 8 and 12 pictures to use.

A fairly large hanging wall clock

Hot glue gun and glue

Poster board cut into a circle just larger than the clock

Ruler

Instructions:

---

1. Find or take 12 pictures with your Mini 8 to use as hour markers.

2. If using a large hanging clock with a flat face, position the pictures at the hour marks and apply hot glue to the backs of the pictures.

3. Affix the pictures to the clock face.

4. If you are using the mechanism of a clock without the face, take the circular piece of poster board and locate the center and draw and X and Y axis with the ruler.

5. Cut out a piece of the center and allow enough room for the mechanism of the clock to fit around it. Apply photos to the four points on the axis and then measure again to

find the other hour marks on the clock face.
Apply the pictures to those spots.

76

Make Your Own Wall Paper

This project will require a lot of Instax photos, but it will also allow you to customize and entire wall with memories and images that you have taken with your Mini 8. This is great for dorm rooms, kid's bedrooms, or really any wall that could use some interesting character.

What you will need:

Your Instax Mini 8 and plenty of film

Enough adhesive squares to cover an entire wall. (This will vary based on the amount of space you want to cover, but one square per photo should be enough.)

Tape measure

Instructions:

1. Once you have determined the size of the wall you want to cover, choose the photos you would like to use.

2. An easy way to measure the wall is to measure the height and width of the space and then multiply those numbers to find the area.

3. The surface area of one Instax mini picture is 7.14 inches. So, to figure out how many pictures will fit on a given space, simply divide the area of the wall by 7.14. This will tell you how many photos will fit.

4. Decide how you want your photos arranged and then affix double sided adhesive squares

to the backs of the photos and affix them to the wall.

Create Frames Out of Instax Photos

This is another project that will help you use your Instax photos as a way to create a useful decorative object. In this case we're going to use Instax photos to create a frame for a larger picture. This is great for large class photos, or any type of group photo.

What you will need:

Your Instax Mini 8 and plenty of film

A large piece of poster board

Glue sticks or hot glue gun

A photo you would like to frame

Instructions:

1. First, center the photo you want to frame on the poster board.

2. Measure 2 inches from the edge of the photo on the poster board on all sides of the photo.

3. Cut the poster board so that a 2-inch boarder is framing the photo.

4. On the horizontal edges of the frame affix your Instax pictures that have been taken in landscape mode.

5. For the vertical edges, use photos that are taken in standard mode. You know how a photo framed with other photos.

6. This is perfect to commemorate an event where you have a large group photo and smaller photos taken with your Mini 8.

Driftwood Hanging Photos

A great way to create a decoration commemorating a special beach vacation is to make a hanging photo arrangement using your Instax photos and a piece of found driftwood. Driftwood has a simple timeless beauty that makes an attractive artistic statement while allowing you to display your personal memories.

What you will need:

Your Instax Mini 8 and plenty of film

A long, thin piece of dry driftwood, about 18-24 inches long.

Enough pieces of medium weight cotton string to hang each picture. The pieces of string can be cut to varying lengths.

Enough mini clothes pin to hang each picture

Instructions:

1. Select the pictures you want to use making sure that it is not too many for the piece of driftwood.

2. Cut the string to varying lengths and tie the ends of each piece to the drift wood, spacing them 3 1/2 to 4 inches apart.

3. Attach the strings to the mini clothes pins and then clip the clothes pins onto the pictures.

4. If you're planning on hanging the wood on a wall you can use small adhesive squares to the backs of each photo and anchor to the

wall in order to keep them stationary.
However, you can also hang them freely.

Create Table Decorations with Instax Photos and Balloons

This is a great way of creating a festive table decoration for parties. It can also be used to make place holders for dining tables. Since this project requires helium filled balloons you will need to visit a party supply store in order to get the balloons. Since helium filled balloons typically do not last very long, we advise getting the balloons as close as possible to your event.

What you will need:

Your Instax Mini 8 and plenty of film

Helium filled balloons

Pieces of cotton string about 3 feet long

Mini adhesive squares

Instructions:

---

1. If you are using this project to make place cards for a party, try to take a picture of all of your guests prior to the event. If using as a general table decoration, simply choose the photos you would like to use.

2. Attach pieces of string to the knot of each balloon.

3. Attach the photos to the strings with the mini adhesive squares. The photo is heavy enough to keep the balloon from floating away, but light enough that is should hover just above a table.

10

Holiday Ideas

The Instax Mini 8 is incredibly useful around the holidays— any holiday! Maybe it's because the Instax Mini 8 makes such a great gift, but also because of how many different projects you can use it for to make every holiday personal and memorable. This section is all about making those special holiday moments all the more special with your Instax Mini 8.

Homemade Christmas Ornaments

Christmas ornaments have special significance to us because as we acquire them they become memories of Christmas' past. Each one holds a story and thanks to your Instax Mini 8 you can start creating your own ornaments that will help create countless new memories. And since Instax film is among the most stable on the market, you can rest assured that your photo ornaments will last for many years to come.

What you will need:

Your Instax Mini 8 and plenty of film

Christmas tree ornament hooks

A small hole punch

Mini adhesive squares

Instructions:

1. Choose which photos you want to use.

2. Punch a small hole at the top of each picture and affix a wire Christmas tree hook.

3. Hang on the tree.

4. If you would like to make double sided ornaments simply punch holes in the photos and attach them to each other, back to back, using the mini adhesive squares.

Halloween Albums

Halloween has always been a favorite holiday for children, but in recent years it has also become a favorite holiday for adults as well. What better way to keep track of all of you Halloween costumes and festivities than with Halloween albums.

What you will need:

Your Instax Mini 8 and plenty of film

Photo albums of any size

Pens or magic markers

Instructions:

---

1. The most important part of this project is taking photos of your friends or family dressed in their Halloween costumes. These albums can be an ongoing project that are added to every year.

2. Choose a picture of each family member in costume and mount to a page in a photo album.

3. On each page, write the year and under each person's picture write their name and what they were dressed as that year.

4. This can also be a great way for adults to commemorate their Halloween parties. Simply snap a photo of each guest as they arrive at the party and then later compile an album that shows what all your friends dressed up as that year.

Personalized Valentine's Day Cards

Valentine's Day is a great time to show those you care about how much you really care. Your Instax Mini 8 is perfect for making custom made valentines for your friends and family. It's also a great project for kids who are going to be bringing valentine's cards for their entire class.

What you will need:

Your Instax Mini 8 and plenty of film

Blank greeting cards or pre-made valentine's cards and envelopes

Colorful magic markers

Double sided tape or glue sticks

Instructions:

1. Take pictures of all of the people you want to make a card for. For kids, have them take pictures of all of the kids in their class.

2. Using the double sided tape or glue stick, affix the pictures to the cards.

3. Using the magic markers, write personalized Valentine's messages on each card.

4. Hand out your cards and show your friends that you really care about them.

Thanksgiving Place Cards

Everyone loves Thanksgiving. Whether it's the time to relax with friends and family, or maybe just the food, Thanksgiving is a time that we all look forward to each year. What better way to surprise the guests at your next Thanksgiving feast than by greeting them at the table with photo place cards courtesy of you Instax Mini 8.

What you will need:

Your Instax Mini 8 and enough film to take pictures of all of your guests

Double sided tape or glue sticks

A magic marker

Blank place cards (available at any stationary store)

Instructions:

1. Using your Mini 8, take a photo of all of your guests. If you can get photos of them before they arrive, even better.

2. Write the person's name at the bottom of each picture.

3. Use the tape or glue sticks to affix the pictures to the blank place cards.

4. Place the cards at the table and wait for your guests to be amazed at your creativity.

Mother's Day Flowers with Instax

Mother's day is a great time to show mom how important she it to you, and it's also a great time to use your Instax Mini 8 to show her just how creative you can be. This year give mom a fun bouquet with a personalized greeting thanks to your Instax Mini 8.

What you will need:

Your Instax Mini 8 to take a picture of yourself

A bouquet of mom's favorite flowers

A blank single panel card

Pens or magic markers

Double sided tape or a glue stick

A piece of colorful ribbon

Hole punch

Instructions:

1. Get someone to snap a photo of you with your Mini 8.

2. Using the tape or glue, affix the picture to the blank card.

3. Decorate the card however you would like.

4. Punch a single hole at the top of the card and thread in the piece of ribbon. Use the ribbon to tie the card around the base of the bouquet.

Father's Day Mini Album

A great way to show dad how much you value his time is to create a mini album of memories. This will require being pretty crafty about getting some shots of dad, but the end result will be sure to make him smile.

What you will need:

Your Instax Mini 8 and plenty of film

A poster board cut into a long strip about 4 inches wide.

Double sided tape or glue stick

Pens or magic markers.

Ruler

Colorful ribbon

Instructions:

---

1. Take lots of pictures with dad.

2. Using your ruler, fold the piece of poster board every three inches so that it has an accordion shape. This will be your album.

3. Affix your photos of dad to each panel of the album using tape or glue and use the empty space around each photo to write a personal message.

4. Fold the album back up and tie with the ribbon. Dad will have a personal memento that is small enough to carry wherever he goes.

Secret Santa with Photos

Secret Santa is a fun holiday activity for the office or school. Using an Instax Mini 8 can make figuring out who your secret Santa is even more fun. The best way to do this project is to make the Mini 8 camera available to the entire office or class and allow everyone to use it to make photo clues.

What you will need:

Your Instax Mini 8 and plenty of film

Instructions:

1. Once you have decided how many gifts everyone will be giving, allow everyone in the office or class to have a chance to take that many pictures to act as clues.

2. These clues should be descriptive enough to allow someone to guess your identity.

3. When it's time to give gifts, attach your clue photo to each gift so that the recipient can guess who their secret Santa might be.

Personalize Gift Tags

This is a great project for parents or anyone who will be giving gifts for holidays or birthdays. It's always fun to see your name on a gift, but it's even more fun to see your picture. Your Instax Mini 8 makes this incredibly easy because Instax pictures are about the same size as a gift tag and they have a space at the bottom to add a message.

What you will need:

Your Instax Mini 8 and plenty of film

Double sided tape

Pens or a magic marker

Instructions:

---

1. Take enough photos of your gift recipients for all of your gifts. Candid shots are great and will end up being a bonus gift.

2. Instead of using conventional gift tags, use the tape to affix each picture to that person's gift.

3. You can use then add a short message to each tag. Then just sit back and watch as everyone looks at the pictures to see which gift is theirs.

Strings of Lights with Instax Photos

This decorative idea is perfect for the holidays, but it can also work as an everyday decoration that will bring light to memories captured with your Instax Mini 8.

What you will need:

Your Instax Mini 8 and plenty of film

Strings of mini lights

Mini clothes pins

Thumb tacks

Instructions:

1. First, take lots of pictures that you want to display in an eye catching way.

2. Using the mini clothes pins, attach the pictures to the strands of lights, spacing them a few inches apart.

3. Hang the lights on a wall with the thumb tacks. Then plug in to enjoy an illuminated photo gallery.

New Year's Resolution Chart

Many of us make New Year's resolutions every, but let's face it, most of us don't keep our resolutions for very long. Luckily, your Instax Mini 8 can help the entire family keep their resolutions by making a handy chart that will be a constant reminder of your goals.

What you will need:

Your Instax Mini 8 and plenty of film

A large poster board

Magic markers

Double sided tape

Instructions:

1. Start by having everyone in the family decide what their resolution is going to be. If your resolution is to hit the gym, take a picture of workout equipment.

2. Divide the poster board into sections so that everyone in the family has a space.

3. Post your picture at the top of your space and then in the space below, keep a log about the progress you're making toward your goals.

11

Kids Party Ideas

Your Instax camera is great for capturing moments at children's parties, but did you know that in addition to snapping pictures of the event, you can use your Mini 8 to create fun activities and party favors that will delight both the kids and their parents. These fun ideas are perfect for any occasion from birthdays to graduations and everything in between. You might even find that some of these ideas are perfect for grown up parties.

Pin the Photo on the Prize

This game takes its inspiration from the classic pin the tail on the donkey. We've replaced the donkey with a chart of prizes and instead of a pin, the kids can use Instax photos of themselves to mark their prize. This way, everyone is sure to be a winner.

What you will need:

Your Instax Mini 8 and plenty of film

A large poster board

A variety of unisex prizes

Double sided tape or adhesive squares

Magic markers

A blindfold

Instructions:

---

1. Start by getting a picture of all the kids at the party.

2. Using the magic markers, section the board into different areas and indicate which prize goes where.

3. Place tape or an adhesive square on each photo and hang the prize board.

4. One by one, allow the kids to be blindfolded, spun around, and given their picture to place on the prize board.

5. After everyone has taken a turn, hand out the prizes.

Take Home Bags with Child's Photo Instead of Name

A take home bag is a staple of kid's parties and usually contains candy and small toys. This project will allow you to make customized bags for each child. This way, at the end of the party they can find their picture and take their bag.

What you will need:

Your Instax Mini 8 and enough film to get a picture of everyone

Festive party bags

Double sided tape

A magic marker

Instructions:

---

1. While the party is happening, use your Mini 8 to snap a picture of each child.

2. Use the magic marker to write the names of all the children on the bags.

3. Affix the pictures of the kids to the bags with tape.

Personalize Cups

Personalizing with the Mini 8 really couldn't be easier considering how fast the pictures come out and how easy they are to attach to almost anything. This is great for kids' parties where it can be difficult to keep track of whose cup belongs to whom and also for grown up parties where all the red cups look the same. Adding a small photo of yourself will ensure that you never pick up the wrong cup again.

What you will need:

Your Instax Mini 8 and enough film for all of your guests

Cups of any type

Double sided tape or mini adhesive squares

Instructions:

1. As your guests arrive, take a picture of them and affix the picture to their cup with tape or an adhesive square.

Fish Pond Game

This modern take on a classic kids' game will provide plenty of fun at parties, but it can also be a fun family activity any time you feel like being creative with your Instax Mini 8. All you have to do is "catch" your picture and you win a prize.

What you will need:

Your Instax Mini 8 and plenty of film

A long stick or rod

A length of string about 3 feet long

Small magnets for the end of the string and back on the pictures

Mini adhesive squares

Small piece of tape

Instructions:

1. If you're using this as a kid's party game, start by taking a picture of all of the kids.

2. Using the adhesive squares, attach a small magnet to each picture.

3. Tie the string to the rod, and attach the magnet to the end of the string with the piece of tape.

4. Lay all of the pictures out in a large grid and allow the kids to take turns using the fishing rod to catch their picture.

Photo Scavenger Hunt

A scavenger hunt is a great idea for a kid's party, but it can be even more fun with an Instax Mini 8. Much like the traditional version of this game, you will be putting together a list of things that the kids will need to find, but instead of rounding up a bunch of hidden objects, why not make the game even more creative by having them "find" the items by taking Instax pictures of them.

What you will need:

An Instax Mini 8 camera and plenty of film

Instructions:

---

1. Start by putting together a list of things for the kids to take pictures of. These can be anything from around the yard or neighborhood.

2. And since the kids aren't actually retrieving the objects, just photographing them, feel free to include things that you would not normally put on a scavenger hunt list.

3. Give the group of kids the camera and send them off to photograph as many of the items as they can.

4. You can either give them a time limit, or simply give them as much time as you'd like.

Customized Cake Topper

This can work either for a kids' party or any type of party that features a cake. We've all seen decorative candles, but why not make you cake even more personalized by creating a custom made cake topper with your Instax Mini 8.

What you will need:

Your Instax Mini 8 and film

2 toothpicks

Double sided tape

Instructions:

---

1. Use you Instax Mini 8 to take two pictures. You can either attempt to take two pictures that are almost identical or you can use two pictures that are very different so that you see a different image depending on which side of the cake you are on.

2. Place one picture face down and apply double sided tape to the back of the picture. Make sure that the tape is placed at the middle of the picture. Put the two toothpick on the tape about an inch apart.

3. On the other picture place double sided tape on the back and then place that picture, face up, on the toothpicks. You now have a double sided topper that can stick right into the top of your cake.

Interactive Party Scrapbook

Scrapbooks are a great way to commemorate your important events and create a story with pictures. Another fun idea for scrapbooking is to let your party guests help create those memories from many different points of view. By allowing everyone a chance to take pictures and turn them in, you can make a scrapbook that everyone had a hand in creating.

What you will need:

Your Instax Mini 8 and plenty of film

A three ring-binder or photo album

Pens or magic markers

Double sided tape of glue sticks

A shoe box or other small box

Instructions:

1. At your party, make your Instax camera available to everyone and encourage them to take pictures throughout the event.

2. Mark a box as the photo drop off box and tell your guests to write their name at the bottom of their photo and drop it in the box.

3. After the party is over, collect all of the photos and start arrange the photos into your album.

4. Now you can see your party from the perspective of all of your guests, and because Instax photos allow you to write a message at

the bottom, you will know who took what picture.

Instax 20 Questions Game

20 questions is a classic party game for kids and adults and you can make it even more fun by using your Instax Mini 8 to capture topics that can be used by your guests.

What you will need:

Your Instax Mini 8 and plenty of film

Permanent marker

Instructions:

---

1. Start by making a list of topics for the game. These can be your classic topics of people, animals, and other objects. Then go out and photograph these things using your Mini 8.

2. Using the permanent marker, label each picture.

3. When playing the game, have one person select a picture and then the other guests have 20 tries to ask questions.

Instax Family Tree

Making a family tree is a great activity for any holiday gathering where the whole family will be together. Since your Instax Mini 8 takes great pictures instantly, it's easy to put together a family tree in no time.

What you will need:

Your Instax Mini 8 and plenty of film

A large poster board

Double sided tape

Pens or magic markers

Instructions:

---

1. Start by taking a photo of everyone in the family.

2. Starting with the older members of the family first, attach the photos to the poster board with the double sided tape. Write their names under their pictures.

3. Then paste pictures of their children to the board and write their names.

4. Keep doing this until you've used everyone's pictures and you have all of the generations represented.

Baby's First Year Album

So much changes in a baby's first year. They grow so quickly, but some family members are sure to miss out on these early developments because they don't live close by. A great way to show everyone the progress your baby is making is to use your Instax Mini 8 to make an album of that special first year.

What you will need:

Your Instax Mini 8 and plenty of film

A photo album or three ring binder

Double sided tape

Pens

Instructions:

1. Starting from just after the baby is born, take a picture once a week to show how the little one is growing and changing.

2. Each week, put a new photo into the album and write the date and number of weeks.

12

School Project Ideas

Your Instax Mini 8 camera can bring fun to pretty much any situation, and school is no different. Spice up everything from textbooks to after school sports with your Instax photos. This section will cover ten amazing ideas for ways you can use you Instax Mini 8 for truly inspired school projects that are fun as well as creative.

Personalize Text Books

Whether you buy or borrow your textbooks, it's a good idea to keep them clean and protected. While there are many ways to cover your books to keep them safe, your Instax Mini 8 will also allow you to make them custom decorated to show your unique personality.

What you will need:

Your Instax Mini 8 and plenty of film

Heavy stock butcher paper (any color you like)

Single sided tape

Double sided tape

Magic markers

Scissors

Instructions:

1. First, we're going to cover your hard cover text books to keep them safe. You're going to want to lay the book open on a large sheet of paper and draw a line around the book about a two inches from the edge of the covers.

2. Use the scissors to cut out the paper cover.

3. Fold the paper around the edges of the book, one edge at a time and use the single sided tape to secure it to the book.

4. When you have taped all of the edges, decide which Instax photos you want to use to decorate the book.

5.   Use a piece of double sided tape to affix your pictures to the book in whatever way you want.

Make Lanyards for School Trips

One of the best parts of school is field trips. But making sure everyone is safe is an important part of making sure the trip goes well. Many schools have students wear a name tag around their neck in the event that a child should get separated from the group. You Instax Mini 8 can do this job even better by including, not just the child's name, but also a recent picture.

What you will need:

Your Instax Mini 8 and enough film to photograph the class

Colored yarn cut into 12 inch lengths (enough for everyone)

A hole punch

Permanent maker

Instructions:

---

1. Start by taking a photo of every child in the class.

2. Use the hole punch to punch a hole at the top of each photo.

3. Thread a length of yard through the hole and tie into a knot.

4. Pass out the name tags to everyone and enjoy a great field trip.

Personalize Your Desk with Instax

Starting a new school year is always a challenge, but thanks to your Instax Mini 8 you can make sure to start off right by customizing your desk to show the class who you really are. From family and pets to summer vacations, use your Instax to tell your class what you've been up to since last year.

What you will need:

Your Instax Mini 8 and plenty of film

Mini adhesive squares

A pen or magic marker

Instructions:

1. First, take lots of pictures of your adventures over the summer.

2. Choose the photos that you want to use to decorate your desk.

3. Using the mini adhesive squares, attach the photos to your desk. The adhesive squares should be easy to remove at the end of the school year.

4. You can also add and modify your photos throughout the year as you take more pictures with your Mini 8.

Student of The Week Chart

Many classrooms have a student of the week honor to single out a student who really went above and beyond academically that week. Since your Instax Mini 8 takes and develops pictures instantly, it's a great way to make a chart showing who really stood out that week.

What you will need:

Your Instax Mini 8 and plenty of film

A large poster board

Magic markers

Double sided tape

Other decorations like glitter pens and stickers

Ruler or yard stick

Instructions:

---

1. Start by making a chart that will have a space for each week of the school year. The easiest way is use a ruler or yard stick to divide the poster board into enough squares so that each week has its own square. Then use a marker or pen to indicate what week it is.

13

Board Decorations

Each week when you choose the student of the week, take a picture of the student, write their name at the bottom of the picture, and use the double sided tape to attach the photo to the poster board.

Bulletin Boards

Bulletin boards can be used for all kinds of things at school and using your Instax Mini 8 is a great way to make them really come alive. From back to school nights to academic progress and announcements, Instax pictures will make your bulletin boards stand out.

What you will need:

Your Instax Mini 8 and plenty of film

Large white boards

White board friendly markers

Double sided tape

Instructions:

---

1. Decide what your bulletin board needs to accomplish. If you are doing a board for back to school night, you can make categories for what topics the class will be covering in the coming school year and take pictures to illustrate those goals.

2. Use the double sided tape to affix Instax pictures to the boards and the white board makers to give explanations.

Flash Cards for Foreign Language

Learning a new language can certainly be a challenge, but your Instax Mini 8 can actually make the process easier. Studies have shown that most of us learn language more quickly when we have a visual reference. Your Mini 8 can help add a visual element to flash cards to make studying much easier.

What you will need:

Your Instax Mini 8 and plenty of film

Index cards

Double sided tape

Pens or magic markers

Instructions:

1. Make a list of words that you want to make flash cards for.

2. Use your Mini 8 to take pictures of all of these words.

3. Tape the pictures to the index cards and write the foreign word under the picture.

4. On the back of the index cards write the translation. This will provide a helpful way to remember difficult words and phrases.

Personalize Cubbies and Lockers

Decorating cubbies and lockers is a fun way to start a new school year, and your Instax Mini 8 is sure to add some extra fun to the process. Take pictures on your summer vacation, activities that you enjoy or really anything you are interested in. For lockers, Instax pictures are a great way to create a DIY wallpaper for the inside.

What you will need:

Your Instax Mini 8 and plenty of film

Mini adhesive squares

Instructions:

1. Use your Instax Mini 8 to take lots of pictures. For cubbies, take a picture of everyone in the class and use the adhesive squares to affix a picture of each child to their cubby.

2. For lockers, use the adhesive squares to stick the Instax photos to the inside of the locker. You can either create a collage, or wallpaper the entire inside of the door.

Use Instax Photos to Make Big Letters

For many different events you might want to create a large sign spelling out the name of a person, place, or activity. Of course, you can buy large letters, but for even more personalized fun, try using your Instax photos to create the letters yourself.

What you will need:

Your Instax Mini 8 and plenty of film

Large pieces of poster board (the size and number of letters will determine how much you need)

Double sided tape

Pens

Ruler

Scissors

Instructions:

1. Once you've decides what words you want to spell out, decide how large you want your letters to be.

2. An easy way to keep all of your letters uniform is to use a ruler to draw two lines on a piece of poster board. This will serve as a guide line much like the lines on a piece of paper.

3. Staying within the guide lines, trace the shape of each letter you need to make. Then use scissors to cut out the letter.

4.   Apply double sided tape to the back of your Instax photos and stick them to the poster board letters. It ok to have a little overlap because you want to cover the poster board as much as possible.

5.   Once you've covered your letters in photos, hang them to create words.

6.   One fun idea is to take photos of things that all start with the letter that you're going to stick them to.

DIY Sports Trading Cards

Trading cards have been a part of sports for over a hundred years because we love to commemorate our favorite players and their statistics. Your Instax Mini 8 can help you create fun homemade trading cards for your whole team. You can keep them or trade them or frame them. Giving out trading cards to the team is a great gift at the end of a season.

What you will need:

Your Instax Mini 8 and plenty of film

Small index cards

Double sided tape

Pens

Instructions:

---

1. Using your Instax Mini 8, take photos of the whole team.

2. Attach the pictures to the index cards with the double sided tape.

3. On the backs of each card write something about each player. This can be about their individual achievements that season, or about an area where they really improved.

Academic Progress Charts

Progress charts are a great way to give students a visual way to see how they are progressing and improving over the course of a school year. Using Instax photos to make the charts even more fun and personal is a surefire way to keep students motivated.

What you will need:

Your Instax Mini 8 and enough film to take a picture of the whole class

Large poster board or bulletin board.

Thumb tacks or double sided tape

Magic markers

Instructions:

1. Take a picture of everyone in the class.

2. Decide what kind of progress you want to chart.

3. Attach the pictures to the board with either tacks or tape depending on what kind of board you are going to use.

4. As the students' progress with their work, move the pictures to show how the students are doing. This will give them a sense of accomplishment as well as a way to visualize their goals.

14

Organizing Ideas

Let's face it, no one like to organize their stuff, but no one likes to be disorganized either. It's hard to be productive when your environment is cluttered, but sometimes getting all of your possessions properly organized just seems like too much of a chore. Thanks to the Intax Mini 8 organizing doesn't have to be an ordeal.

Organize Boxes with Instax

This is especially helpful for moving, but it can also be a valuable idea for keeping track of things that are stored in boxes around the house. Your Instax photos are small yet durable so you will be able to see what's in your boxes for years to come.

What you will need:

Your Instax Mini 8 and plenty of film

Double sided tape or adhesive squares

Permanent markers

Instructions:

---

1. Start by taking a picture of what is in each box. For moving, you can take a picture of your dishes before they go into a box and then using the tape or adhesive squares, attach the picture to the box so that when you arrive at your new home you will be able to see exactly what is in each box.

Organize Shoes with Instax

Most people these days own numerous pairs of shoes, and many of us have closets filled with shoe boxes containing these shoes. The problem is that in order to find a specific pair, you might have to dig through box after box to find what you are looking for. Luckily, your Instax Mini 8 is perfect for keeping track of every pair so that you will simply have to glance at each box in order to see what is inside.

What you will need:

Your Instax Mini 8 and enough film to take pictures of all of your shoes

Double sided tape

A pen

Instructions:

1. Start by taking a picture of every pair of shoes you own.

2. As you put the shoes back in their boxes, write the type of shoe on the blank spot at the bottom of its picture.

3. Tape each picture to the corresponding shoe box and put all of the boxes back in storage. Now when you need to find a specific pair you just need to look at the pictures to see what is inside.

Plan your Outfits with Instax

If you have a busy schedule like most people, picking out clothes every day is just one more thing to do before heading out the door. Instead of staring at a closet full of clothes every morning, use your Instax Mini 8 to help organize your wardrobe for easy and attractive outfits every day. In addition to this being a great way to avoid before work stress, it can also be a fun activity with the kids for picking outfits for the next school day.

What you will need:

Your Instax Mini 8 and plenty of film

All the clothing you wear for work or school

Permanent markers

Small cork board

Thumb tacks

Instructions:

1. Start by using your Mini 8 to take pictures of all of the shirts, pants, skirts, and dresses you generally wear to work of school. Once you've done this, you're ready to mix and match.

2. At the bottom of each picture, label with the name of the piece of clothing. ie: blue skirt, or red short-sleeve shirt.

3. Divide all of the pictures into categories.

4. To assemble outfits, post a picture from each category to the cork board to see how well they go together. You can also make groups

of pictures to create outfits that you know will work. This can be a fun way to allow kids to participate in choosing their own clothes without having to be surprised by their choices right before heading out for the day.

Store your Photos in Used Cartridges

Most of the ideas we've explored so far are either about how to use the Mini 8 in fun ways, or how to create fun projects with the pictures. But now we're going to cover a great way to keep your Instax pictures safe for storage.

What you will need:

Your Instax pictures

Used Instax film cartridges

Instructions:

1. Once you've used up a cartridge of Instax film you might think that tossing it in the recycling bin is the only option. Amazingly, your used Instax cartridges make the perfect DIY storage for your precious Instax pictures.

2. Once the cartridge is empty, simply slide your pictures back into the cartridge for easy storage. The durable construction of the cartridge will keep your pictures safe, and this way they don't end up becoming trash.

Garden Journal

Having your own garden is a great way to eat healthy and feel connected to the earth. Once everything is planted, however, it can be a challenge to keep track of what you're growing. By using your Instax Mini 8 to keep a garden journal you can, not only keep track of what is currently growing, you can also keep a record of what you have grown in the past so that you know what works best in your garden.

What you will need:

Your Instax Mini 8 and plenty of film

A three ring binder with stiff pages

Double sided tape

Pens

Instructions:

1. Once you've planted your garden and the things are starting to grow, take pictures of every different plant.

2. Using the tape, affix the pictures to the pages of the binder and label it.

3. As the plants continue to grow you can take "status update" pictures of everything to see what kind of progress they are making.

4. In future years you can then look back to see what you grew, and how well it progressed in your garden.

Create To-Do Lists

This is a great way to encourage the entire family to pitch in and help with the chores. Your Instax Mini 8 will allow you to visualize all of the day to day tasks that need to be accomplished and make it easy to see which member of the family is responsible for it.

What you will need:

Your Instax Mini 8 and plenty of film

A large poster board

Magic makers

Double sided tape

Instructions:

---

1. Start by making a list of all of the chores that need to be accomplished on a regular basis.

2. Take a picture that represents each of these tasks. For instance, take a picture of the washer and dryer to signify doing the laundry.

3. Take a picture of each family member.

4. On the poster board, plot out a space for each task.

5. Using the double sided tape, affix the pictures of the tasks to the board.

6. Then decide who will do each project and paste their picture next to that task. Now everyone can get to work and all of the tasks will be completed.

Organize Binders and Photo Albums

Keeping albums and binder organized can be difficult unless you want to open each on to see what is in there. Luckily, your Instax Mini 8 can take all of the guess work out so you can easily reach for what you need.

What you will need:

Your Instax Mini 8 and plenty of film

All of your photo albums or binders

A pen or permanent marker

Adhesive squares

Instructions:

1. Start by getting all of your albums or binder together, and make a list of what each one contains.

2. Go take pictures of things that will correspond with what is in all of the binders.

3. Use the adhesive squares to affix the spines of the binders and attach the pictures. Now you can tell at a glance what is in each album.

Artsy Labels for Cabinets

Much like organizing all of your albums, cabinets can be prone to clutter as well. Thankfully, your Instax Mini 8 can help create helpful and fun labels for cabinets. Indulge your artistic side by finding images with your Mini 8 to make cabinet doors really pop.

What you will need:

Your Instax Mini 8 and plenty of film

Adhesive squares

Permanent marker

Instructions:

1. Start by identifying what is in the cabinets that you want to label.

2. Go out and take creative images using your Mini 8.

3. At the bottom of each picture write a helpful label or message.

4. Using the adhesive squares, affix each picture to its corresponding cabinet.

Customized Mini Photo Boxes

These small mini photo boxes are a great way to store your photos, but they also work as a great way to package photos as a gift. Make customized boxes and fill them with photos from event, birthdays, parties, weddings, or any occasion that you want to commemorate with a unique gift.

What you will need:

Your Instax Mini 8 and plenty of film

Empty metal mint boxes. Altoid boxes are perfect.

Strong hold glue

Permanent marker

Instructions:

1. Using your Mini 8 take pictures that you would like to turn into a gift.

2. Choose one photo to be your cover photo. This will the the picture on the outside of the box.

3. Using the glue, affix the cover photo to the top of the box. Use the marker to write a message on the cover photo.

4. Fill the box with the rest of the photos and present as a great personalized gift.

Keep Track of Birthdays

Without hectic schedules, it can sometimes be difficult to keep track of specific dates, but your Instax Mini 8 will help by making a customized calendar to help you remember those special days.

What you will need:

Your Instax Mini 8 and plenty of film

A large blank calendar

Permanent marker

Double sided tape

Instructions:

1. Using your Instax Mini 8, take a picture of all of the people whose birthdays you want to keep track of.

2. On the calendar, write down whose birthday is on what day.

3. Using the double sided tape, affix the photo of each person to their birthday on the calendar.

4. Hand the calendar in a prominent place so that you can easily glance at it to see if there are any birthdays coming up.

16

Art Project Ideas

The Instax Mini 8 is designed specifically to let you be creative anywhere and at any time. The freedom to take, develop, and view your pictures instantly gives you the freedom to let your creativity shine no matter where you are. This section will cover ideas for making unique and timeless art projects using your Mini 8. These ideas can be used as decorations, gifts, or in whatever way you want.

Create a Hanging Mobile

A homemade mobile is a great decoration for any room, not just kid's rooms. You can use some simple crafting materials and your Instax photos to create mobiles that will show off your best Instax photos and make an interesting conversation piece.

What you will need:

Your Instax Mini 8

6 pieces of medium strength metal wire (about the thickness of a clothes hanger)

5 pieces of cotton string in varying lengths

6 pieces of cotton string two inches' long

6 Instax photos

Single hole punch

Instructions:

1. Start by choosing the photos you want to use. You will need six.

2. Punch holes in the top of each picture.

3. Build the mobile by starting with one piece of wire. Tie one piece of string to each end and tie the other ends of those string to other pieces of wire. Repeat this until you have used all of the wire and longer pieces of string.

4. Tie your Instax photos to the two inch pieces of string and tie those strings to the ends of the hanging wires.

Create Fun Personal Bookmarks

One of the simplest uses for Instax pictures is as bookmarks. One fun idea for bookmarks is to make them reading themed. Take pictures of you, your children, or friends reading their favorite books and then gift them the picture as a bookmark.

What you will need:

Your Instax Mini 8 and plenty of film

Permanent marker

Instructions:

---

1. There really aren't any rules about what kinds of photos to take for bookmarks, but once you've decided on the photo, write a personal message at the bottom and give as a gift. This can be a great way to encourage kids to read.

Write Books and Illustrate with Instax

Writing is truly one of the most valuable skills a person can have, and learning to write should start as early as possible. Since we're all natural story tellers, it makes sense to start telling stories as soon as we can. By allowing your children to write stories that can be illustrated with your Instax Mini 8 you're giving them a huge head start in the world.

What you will need:

Your Instax Mini 8 and plenty of film

A composition book or notebook

Pens

Double sided tape

Instructions:

1. Start by figuring out the story. The best way to start writing a story is to tell it out loud.

2. Once you're happy with it, write it down in the composition book. Be sure to not put too much text on each page. Spread it out so you have lots of room for you Instax Illustrations.

3. Once the story is written down, go out and take picture that will go along with what you've written.

4. You might try staging some scenes and taking pictures of that, or you could simply photograph what you see in the world.

5.   When you have enough pictures to illustrate
      your book, apply double sided tape to the
      backs of the pictures and affix them to the
      appropriate pages.

Memory Game

The classic memory game is a great way to instill memory skills while still having fun. The idea is to make a grid of cards all face down. For each card there is a match. The point of the game is to remember which card is where and to flip one over and try to remember where its match is. This is a great way to use you Instax Mini 8

What you will need:

Your Instax Mini 8 and plenty of film

Instructions:

1. First, decide how many pairs you want to make. For a challenging game, 15 to 20 pairs is recommended.

2. Go out and take pictures of different things using your Mini 8. Remember that you need to take two pictures of everything in order to make matches. So if you want to take a picture of a tree, take the same picture twice.

3. Once you have all of your matches it's time to play the game. Shuffle all of the photos and spread all of the pictures on a table face down. Arrange them in a grid. The first player will turn over one picture. Then they will turn over another picture. If the pictures do not match, turn both pictures face down again.

4. When you find a matching pair of photos, pick them up and keep them in a pile. The

player with the most pairs of photos at the end wins.

Bird Watcher's Journal

Spending time in nature is one of life's simplest pleasures, and exploring your environment while looking for indigenous birds can be a peaceful way of communing with the world around you. Since your Instax Mini 8 is perfect for all kinds of wilderness treks, it only makes sense to use it to create a bird watching journal.

What you will need:

Your Instax Mini 8 and plenty of film

A binder with pages or notebook

Double sided tape

Pens

Instructions:

1. Take a walk in nature and use your Mini 8 to snap pictures of the different birds in your area.

2. After your walk in the woods, spend some time identifying the birds you've photographed. Write the name of each one at the bottom of each picture.

3. Using the double sided tape, affix your photos to the notebook and make a note of the date and location where you saw each bird.

Create Your Own Labels

You can certainly buy store bought labels for things like jams but if you're planning on giving away the fruits of your labors as gifts, wouldn't it be more personal to make your own custom labels?

What you will need:

Your Instax Mini 8 and plenty of film

Gifts like jars of jam, preserves, or a special bottle of wine

Double sided tape

Pens

Instructions:

---

1. Choose the photos you want to use and pair them with a gift. Let's say it's a jar of homemade orange marmalade.

2. Write a short message on the bottom of the Instax photo and affix it to the jar using the double sided tape.

30-Day Photo Challenge

This is a fun project that doesn't just have to be for social media. It's a bit like a scavenger hunt, but more personal, and the end result is a mini album that reflects the different subject you have been seeking out over the course of a month.

What you will need:

Your Instax Mini 8 and plenty of film

A notebook

Pens

Instructions:

1. This is more of a challenge than a project so feel free to make your list a little difficult. The first step is to number a page 1 to 30.

2. Then decide what 30 things you would like to take pictures of. You will be taking one picture every day so make sure it's something that you can find, but don't make it too easy.

3. Once you have chosen your plan for the month, take time every day to seek out that item on your list and photograph it with your Mini 8.

4. After you've crossed off every item on your list, feel free to make a mini album that reflects the month you just had.

Instax Branch Display

A vase full of long willow branches can be an elegant decorative touch to almost any room. It also helps bring a bit of nature into the house but doesn't require much maintenance. Using your Instax Mini 8 you can take this idea one step further by using your Instax pictures.

What you will need:

Your Instax Mini 8 and plenty of film

About 10 long branches

A large vase

A small piece of string (about 3 to 4 inches long) for each photo you want to use

Hole punch

Instructions:

1. Start by choosing the photos you want to use. If you're going to make a large display you will probably want to choose quite a few photos.

2. Punch a hole at the top of each picture and tie one end of a string to each one.

3. Lay the branches on the floor and tie several pictures to each branch.

4. One by one, place the branches into the vase and arrange so that they spread out.

5. For an extra artistic touch, try painting all of the branches a certain color before attaching photos.

DIY Wall Art

Instax photos are perfect for creating fun and eye catching wall art. It's also a great way to make use of old frames that are collecting dust. You can choose your photos however you want but we suggest deciding on a theme for each framed art project. Something like a special vacation, wedding, or graduation.

What you will need:

Your collection of your Instax prints divided into categories

Large picture frame with no back

White paper cut to the size of the frame

Double sided tape

Craft glue

Instructions:

1. Start by choosing the photos you want to use. The theme is totally up to you.

2. Apply pieces of double sided tape to the backs of each photo and arrange them on the sheet of paper however you like. Some people prefer to make a pattern, but grids of photos are fine as well.

3. Apply a small amount of glue to the edge of the sheet of paper and then press it into the frame. Allow ample time to dry.

4. Your wall art is now ready to hang.

Instax House Tour

This is a fun art project that adds a unique insight into your home. While it is great for housewarming parties, it is also a wonderful reminder of when you first moved into a new home.

What you will need:

Your Instax Mini 8 and plenty of film

A large wooden picture frame

A sheet of cork board as large as the picture frame

Flat head metal thumb tacks

Instructions:

---

1. Start by taking pictures throughout your home. You can include people in these photos. Just keep in mind that you will need enough photos to completely fill the center of the picture frame.

2. Once you have all of your photos, lay the cork board on a table or floor and start attaching the photos.

3. To attach the photos, place one in the top corner of the cork board and press a thumb tack just next to it so that the flat top of the thumb tack holds it in place. Do not pierce the photo with the tack itself.

4. Then, place another photo next to the first one and push another tack between them so that the top of that tack holds both photos.

5. Continue doing this until you have filled the entire picture frame.

6. Once the cork board is full of photos, use several more tacks to attach the cork board to the back of the picture frame. It is now ready to display.

Instax Business Cards

Everyone needs a business card, but these days it has become difficult to stand out from the pack. Thanks to Instax, you can create your own unique business cards that will be eye catching and memorable to everyone who receives one.

What you will need:

Your Instax Mini 8 and plenty of film

Fine tipped permanent marker

Instructions:

1. For this project you will need to enlist the help of a friend to take a number of pictures of you.

2. Start by deciding how many business cards you want to make and then have a friend take that many Instax photos of you.

3. At the bottom of each photo write your name, phone number, and if you want, your email address using permanent marker.

4. Then hand them out and watch as people see just how interesting and creative you must be. These cards will ensure that you always stand out from the pack.

17

Fun Around the House

The main purpose of your Instax Mini 8 is having fun. From capturing candid moments to creating unique art projects, the important thing is that your Mini 8 brings you together with your friends and family so that you can share these moments with each other. This section will focus on ideas for having fun around the house anytime.

Height Charts for The Kids

Most houses with small children will feature a height chart for the kids. This is usually just a series of marks and dates on a door frame to show how much and how fast the kids are growing. With your Instax Mini 8 you can take this activity one step further by showing their growth progress with Instax photos.

What you will need:

Your Instax Mini 8 and plenty of film

Thumb tacks

A pen

Tape measure

Instructions:

1. Kids grow pretty fast so it's a good idea to update your height chart every six months or so. Start by having each child stand against a wall or door frame and mark their height with a pen or pencil.

2. Take a photo of the child and, using a thumb tack, attach the photo to the wall so that the top edge of the photo is at the exact point where you measured their height.

3. Every few months repeat this. You will not only see how tall the kids are getting, but you will also have a photo of them when they were that height. You can even use the blank space at the bottom of the photos to note the child's height and date when they were measured.

Create Your Own Cook Books

Cooking is a great family activity that allows you to share your recipes with the people you care about. Thanks to your Instax Mini 8 you can also create custom cook books to pass along to anyone who loves eating your food.

What you will need:

Your Instax Mini 8 and plenty of film

A three ring binder with lots of pages

Double sided tape

Pens

Instructions:

---

1. This isn't a project that needs to be done all at once. But you can start by simply choosing a meal that you would like to include.

2. First, take a picture of all of the ingredients and listing them on a page in the binder. Use the double sided tape to paste the picture next to the ingredients.

3. As you go through the steps of cooking your meal, take pictures that show what you are doing. Write out the instructions in the binder and tape the photos next to the instructions.

4. When you have a completed meal, take a photo of the finished product and tape that at the end of your recipe in the binder. Continue doing this when you make different meals

and over time you will compile a
photographic book of all of your recipes.

5.   Note: To make books for multiple people,
take multiple photos of each step and then
assemble the books separately.

Create Your Own Baby Books

Baby books are a great way to keep the memories of your kids during their first years of life. From their birth, to first steps and first words, a baby book will be a timeless reminder of those special times. Your Instax Mini 8 is perfect for keeping this record for many years to come.

What you will need:

Your Instax Mini 8 and plenty of film

A large photo album

Colorful pens or markers

Instructions:

---

1. The most important part of this project is the photos you take. Make sure you have your Mini 8 on hand so that you can document all of your special moments.

2. This is meant to be an ongoing project so as your child continues to grow, keep taking photos of their milestone moments and whenever you have a new photo, paste it into the album and write a short message about what happened and the date.

3. Over the course of a few years you will have compiled an album of unforgettable moments that you can treasure forever.

Create Fun Refrigerator Magnets

This is a fun activity to make magnets for your own refrigerator or as gifts for friends and family. Refrigerator magnets are fun and useful so why not use your Mini 8 to make custom magnets?

What your will need:

Your Instax Mini 8 and plenty of film

Small low profile magnets

Craft glue

Instructions:

1. Take lots of pictures with your Mini 8 and choose the ones you want to make into magnets.

2. Using craft glue, attach the magnets to the backs of the photos and allow to dry.

3. You can even write a little message at the bottom of each picture.

Make Chore Charts Fun with Instax Photos

Let's face it, no one likes to do chores, but your Instax Mini 8 can make the whole process a lot more fun by allowing you to make chore charts that make choosing and completing tasks more like a game and less like a... Well, a chore.

What you will need:

Your Instax Mini 8 and plenty of film

A large poster board

Magic markers

Velcro strips

Instructions:

---

1. Take a photo of everyone in the family with your Mini 8.

2. On the poster board, write out all of the chores that need to be accomplished every week.

3. Attach one side of the velcro to each picture and the other side to the space next to one of the chores.

4. Now it's time for everyone to place their picture next to a chore. You can determine the order of choosing by a lottery or simply change the chores weekly yourself.

Personalize Bedroom Doors

This is a fun project that can be an ongoing decoration activity for the whole family. Your Instax Mini 8 is perfect for snapping fun pictures to use and the blank spaces at the bottom of the pictures allow you to write fun messages to anyone passing by.

What your will need:

Your Instax Mini 8 and plenty of film

Double sided tape or adhesive squares

Magic markers

Instructions:

---

1. Start by having fun taking lots of Instax photos to use.

2. Use the double sided tape or adhesive squares to attach the photos to your door. You can arrange them in whatever patterns you want.

3. Write messages on the blank spaces beneath the photos.

Puppy/Kitten Book

This is a great project for the whole family after the arrival of a new puppy or kitten. Much like a baby book for a new baby, creating a record of the growth and development of a furry new member of the family is a great way to keep those memories for years to come.

What you will need:

Your Instax Mini 8 and plenty of film

An album

Double sided tape

Magic markers

Instructions:

---

4. When a new puppy or kitten arrives it's only natural to want to take lots of photos of them.

5. Since Instax pictures have a space at the bottom to write notes, you can make a note of when the photo was taken and what you were doing. You could take pictures of a first trip to the park, or a first visit to grandma's house.

6. As you take pictures, put them in the album using the double sided tape, and make more notes about what was happening when the pictures were taken.

Baby Bump Chart

Your Instax Mini 8 is a great way to document the progress on your pregnancy even before the baby comes. Many people are keeping a record of how their bump is growing as the pregnancy progresses, and your Instax Mini 8 is perfect for taking quick photos.

What you will need:

Your Instax Mini 8 and plenty of film

A large poster board

Double sided tape

Pens or magic markers

Ruler

Instructions:

---

1. A normal pregnancy lasts forty weeks, so first use a ruler to divide your poster board into 40 spaces large enough so that you can post an Instax photo.

2. Each week take a photo of yourself in profile so that you can see how your bump is growing.

3. After taking the picture, post it on the poster board space for that week and when the baby comes you will be able to see your progress every week for your entire pregnancy.

Workout Progress Chart

This progress chart is similar to the baby bump progress chart but it doesn't have t be limited to a number of weeks. If you have a specific goal in mind you can make your chart reflect that goal, but otherwise you can keep track of your progress for as long as you want. This can be a great motivational tool because you will be able to look back at past pictures and see that you have, indeed, been making great progress.

What you will need:

Your Instax Mini 8 and plenty of film

A large poster board

Double sided tape

Pens or magic markers

Ruler

Instructions:

---

1. Start by using a ruler to divide your poster board into individual spaces for posting pictures.

2. At the end of every week take a picture of yourself to see how your body is changing due to your new workout regimen.

3. Post the pictures to the poster board in order and over time you will be able to see your progress and keep track of exactly how quickly you've been progressing.

Framed Letters

This fun project will allow you to create an art project that can spell out anything you want using your Instax photos. It can be a wonderful home decoration or an unexpected gift for friends or family. You can spell whatever you want but for this demonstration we're going to make a decoration that spells LOVE with one letter contained in each frame.

What you will need:

Your Instax Mini 8 and plenty of film

4 picture frames roughly 12 inches tall and 8 inches' wide

4 plain white pieces of paper

Double sided tape

Instructions:

1. Choose the photos you want to use. Each letter will require about 8 to 10 Instax photos.

2. Apply double sided tape to the backs of the photos. Paste the photos to the pieces of paper so that they spell out the four letters.

3. Insert the papers into the frames and hang so that the word is spelled out.

18

Gift Ideas

The Instax Mini 8 makes a great gift, but you can also use your Mini 8 to make gifts for other people. This section will cover a wide variety of gift idea that are sure to be personal and thoughtful for the many special people in your life. Feel free to explore with different variation on these ideas, and above all be creative.

Personalized Cards for Any Occasion

Greeting cards have become a part of practically every holiday and occasion, but what if you could personalize all of your cards so that everyone on your list felt as though you took the time to craft something just for them.

What you will need:

Your Instax Mini 8 and plenty of film

Blank greeting cards and envelopes (can be found at any stationary store)

Double sided tape

Pen

Instructions:

1. Start by choosing the photo or photos you want to use. The style may depend on the person or the occasion.

2. Use the double sided tape to affix the photos to the front and/or inside of the card.

3. Write a personal message on the front or inside of the card. Seal the card in an envelope.

Books for Grandparents

This idea can serve to commemorate the birth of a child or simply a gift from a child to their grandparents. As a gift from an older child to their grandparents, this can be a story book that uses Instax photos as illustrations.

What you will need:

Your Instax Mini 8 and plenty of film

A composition book or paper bound in a report binder

Colored pencils or magic markers

Double sided tape

Instructions:

---

1. First decide what kind of book this will be. If it is a story book from children to their grandparents decide what the story will be, and using pens write the story into the book.

2. Once you have the story, go out and use your Mini 8 to take pictures that will illustrate your story.

3. Once you have the pictures you need, use the double sided tape to affix the pictures to the pages of the book.

4. If you're going to do a commemorative book, use photos you've taken of your new baby and on each page, include a photo or two and some text about where the photo was taken and how old the baby was in each photo.

Either way, this will be a cherished gift that any grandparent would be happy to receive.

DIY Flip Books

For a simple way to add a little animation to your art projects try this fun Instax challenge. It makes a great gift for any occasion, and will allow you to express your true creative nature.

What you will need:

Your Instax Mini 8 and plenty of film
Small stapler

Instructions:

---

1. This one is a little challenging, but with a little practice you should be able to master it. Start by deciding on a very simple scene you want to shoot. Maybe just you waving at the camera.

2. First, position yourself with one hand raised. Take a picture in landscape mode, and then move your hand slightly. Take another picture and continue moving your hand slightly and taking pictures until you have run out of film.

3. Staple all of the photos together. You can use the blank white space on the film. When you flip through the photos you will become animated and it should look like you are waving.

4. This basic idea can be used to capture a wide variety of motions. Really anything will work as long as you can start and stop the motion between taking photos.

Framed Photos

Framed photos are a wonderful gift for any occasion. Your Instax photos allow you to make frames in a variety of ways using a variety of materials. You can either frame photos individually, or group them together and frame them. It's really up to you. This is an easy way to take virtually any type of cardboard and turn it into a cool frame for your photos.

What you will need:

Your Instax Mini 8 and plenty of film

2 pieces of cardboard (you can use any type or color but they should be the same size)

Crafting knife

Adhesive squares

Pen

Instructions:

---

1. Choose the photos you want to frame. If you're going to frame individual pictures, first measure the size of the picture not including the blank space at the bottom.

2. Use a pen to trace the shape of the picture onto one or the pieces of cardboard.

3. Use the crafting knife to cut out that shape.

4. Attach the photo to the other piece of cardboard with an adhesive square, then attach that to the frame you have already cut out.

DIY Mini Photo Albums

A mini photo album can be a great way to keep some special photos with you on the go. It also makes a perfect sentimental gift for anyone. This album is modeled on the folding wallet style photo albums, but made specifically for your Instax photos.

What you will need:

Your Instax Mini 8 and plenty of film

Strip of card board 4 inches wide and 12 inches long

Double sided tape

Instructions:

---

1. Start by choosing the photos you want to use based on whom you are giving them to.

2. Apply double sided tape to the first photo and place it on the cardboard strip all the way to the left. Fold the cardboard right at the edge of the photo and apply another photo to the opposite side.

3. Repeat this until you have run out of room on the cardboard. You can make a longer album but the longer it is, the thicker it will be as well.

Personalize Gift Bags

Gift bags are a great option when you don't want to wrap is gift in the traditional fashion. Gifts like wine are difficult to wrap, so a bag makes much more sense. Thanks to your Mini 8 you can personalize your bags for any occasion.

What you will need:

Your Instax photos

Gift bags of any kind

Adhesive squares

Instructions:

---

1. Once you've chosen the photos you want to use, simply affix them to the bags with the adhesive squares. These will work better than double sided tape because many gift bags are made of glossy paper.

Make Mini Photo Holders

A great way to make minimalist photo holders for you Instax photos is to use old fashioned binder clips because not only do they hold small photos without damaging them, but when closed they will stand up. This gift is perfect for displaying photos on any surface and since they open and close so easily, you can always change the photos that you currently have on display.

What you will need:

Your Instax photos

Binder clips

Instructions:

1. Once you've chosen the photos you want to use, simply close the wire parts of the binder clips so that it firmly holds the photo. In this position you can use the base of the clip as a stand.

Custom Wrapping Paper

This customized wrapping paper is a gift in itself. Instead of traditional wrapping paper that is generally thrown away, you will have bonus gifts in the form of Instax photos which can then be removed and displayed elsewhere.

What you will need:

Your Instax photos

Wrapping paper

Double sided tape

Instructions:

---

1. Start by choosing which photos you want to use.

2. Wrap the gift.

3. Apply double sided tape to the backs of the photos and attach them to the wrapped package.

Instax Heart Shaped Collage

This is a great way to use your Instax photos to make a beautiful eye catching decoration that also makes the perfect gift. The heart shape is a perfect complement to any room of the house, but upon closer examination, you will see that the heart is made up of individual Instax photos that you can choose to fit any theme.

What your will need:

Your Instax Mini 8 and plenty of film

Medium sized cork board

Flat head thumb tacks

Instructions:

1. First, decide what you want your theme to be. Once you have an idea, go out and take lots of photos with your Mini 8 that will fit your theme.

2. Once you have your photos, arrange some of them on the cork board so that they form the shape of a heart. It's ok if they overlap. Use the thumb tacks to attach them to the cork board.

3. Then, fill in the heart with the rest of your photos, using tacks to attach them to the board as you go.

Give Someone Else the Camera!

By this point, you've been having a lot of fun trying all of the things your Instax Mini 8 can do. From creative art projects that give your home a special, personal feel, to practical projects that help make your day easier, the Instax Mini 8 is so versatile and easy to use, the possibilities are practically limitless. Since you have, no doubt, become a fan of all things Instax, our final suggestion is to share your experiences by giving someone else an Instax Mini 8. You can lend them your camera to explore the world of instant photography, or you can buy them their own camera as a gift that is sure to be treasured for years to come. Because Instax cameras are perfect for the whole family, and they are a wonderful way to bring family and friends together so that you can all take part in creating memories that will last forever.

8

Bonus Special Effect

Double Exposure

This bonus feature of the Instax Mini 8 is a bit of a hack and it might take a little practice, but once you've mastered the technique you will be able to make out of this world photos thanks to a double exposure. All film cameras work on the same basic principle. Light enters the lens and exposes a piece of film. If the film is exposed for too long, the picture comes out too light. If the exposure isn't long enough, the picture will be too dark. Luckily, your Instax Mini 8 is designed to know exactly how much light is necessary for perfect pictures.

One advanced technique often used by professional photographers to produce surreal images is to expose the film twice, capturing two different images on the same piece of film. With a little wizardry, you can achieve this cool effect with your Mini 8. Just follow these simple steps.

POP OPEN THE BACK DOOR THAT REVEALS THE FILM CARTRIDGE.

Aim, adjust flash, and take your shot!

Before the camera's mechanism has a chance to eject the photo, tip out the film cartridge (pull it backward toward yourself) just a bit.

Then push the cartridge back in when the camera has done its mechanical whirling sounds. This way, the photo will not get pushed out, but it will have been exposed to the shot.

NOTE: Don't pull the cartridge all the way out of the camera, or else light will get into the camera body and your photo will turn out completely white.

Close the back door.

Retake your photo, as you normally would, letting the photo pop out.

When the photo develops you will notice that one image is superimposed on the other. You can experiment with all kinds of double exposures and figure out how to get the perfect lighting. Then go out and impress your friends with your expertise using the Instax Mini 8.

Next Steps...

DID YOU ENJOY THE BOOK?

IF SO, THEN LET ME KNOW BY LEAVING A REVIEW ON AMAZON! Reviews are the lifeblood of independent authors. I would appreciate even a few words and rating if that's all you have time for. Here's the link:

http://www.healthyhappyfoodie.org/v1-freebooks

IF YOU DID NOT LIKE THIS BOOK, THEN PLEASE TELL ME! Email me at feedback@HHFpress.com and let me know what you didn't like! Perhaps I can change it. In today's world a book doesn't have to be stagnant, it can improve with time and feedback from readers like you. You can impact this book, and I welcome your feedback. Help make this book better for everyone!

DO YOU LIKE FREE BOOKS?

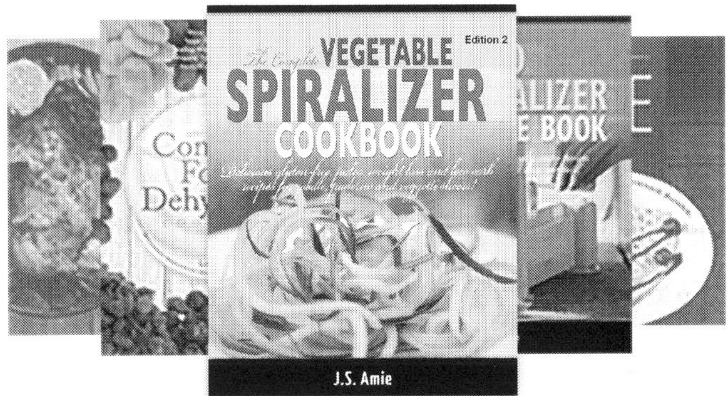

Every month we release a new book, and we offer it to our current readers first...absolutely free! This helps us get early feedback before launching a book, and lets you stock your shelf full of interesting and valuable books for free!

Some recent titles include:

- The Complete Vegetable Spiralizer Cookbook
- My Lodge Cast Iron Skillet Cookbook
- 101 The New Crepes Cookbook

To receive this month's free book, just go to

http://www.healthyhappyfoodie.org/v1-freebooks

20517424R00103

Printed in Great Britain
by Amazon